One Name
One Number

The Story of *Living Hope Ministries*

By
Richard Brunton
with Pam Weaver

ISBN: 978-1-907636-39-4

Published by Verité CM Ltd for *Living Hope Ministries*
Lancing, West Sussex, United Kingdom BN15 OHF
www.living-hope.org.uk
email: lhm@living-hope.org.uk

British Library Cataloguing Data
A catalogue record of this book is available from
The British Library

Typesetting and production management by
Verité CM Ltd, Worthing, West Sussex UK
+44 (0) 1903 241975
Printed in England

Dedication

This book is dedicated to my wife, Elaine. Her love for me and her dedication to our Lord Jesus expressed in her willingness to let me do the will of God are exemplary. Sometimes when her health was not so good, she still urged me to press on. Her counsel and wisdom have been remarkable too. Her care of the family is outstanding. Each of our sons and now daughters- in- law have all played their part in loving support.

So many friends have contributed so richly into my life and the danger of mentioning some is that so many will be missed out. Suffice it to say that friends from early years, college years, teaching years, first pastorate, Brighton years, Lancing years and since 1994, *Living Hope Ministries* years have all helped, encouraged, corrected and prayed. Thank you all so very much.

A special thank you to Pam Weaver whose inspiration and hard work has helped put into print what otherwise would have remained in my head. Our motivation is that so many ordinary people can be greatly used of God if we trust and obey. Do not give up, keep looking to Jesus.

My thanks to David Weaver and Bernard Lord for the use of their photographs, also to Vivien Hawkins and Helen Bryant who acted as proof-readers.

Living Hope Ministries was birthed when the word 'Hope' was far away in the distance. The faithfulness of God has become a living reality in this world-wide ministry of Jesus Christ. You will be thoroughly blessed as you read through these pages. Your hope will be brighter and your faith richer in Jesus.

Rev. Major Sam & Mrs. Sophie Larbie – Senior Pastor of Elim Camberwell

Richard has a passion for the lost and for missions. His anointing and humility have already achieved great things in many nations in such a short period of time as his vision for Living Hope grows.

Pete Light – Senior Pastor of New life Church Romsey

Living Hope is a compelling story; honest, personal and glorifying to God.

John Woods – Senior Pastor of Lancing Tabernacle

Living Hope Ministries is a remarkable story of the Lord's grace and favour seen in action – not just to the nations across the world, but in the local churches of the UK – encouraging and assisting congregations large and small in true apostolic spirit.

Rev. Ray Orr – Senior Pastor Shoreham Baptist Church

The story of how Living Hope Ministries was born and has grown and developed is, above all, the story of how God can use ordinary people like us to do extraordinary things. Read this inspiring story and be encouraged in your own adventures of faith!

Graham Jefferson – recently retired senior Pastor of New Life Durrington

This is an inspiring story of a truly pioneering ministry. While fully contemporary, it has echoes of the past missionary endeavours of those Christians who opened up new continents to the gospel. Richard's passion for equipping pastors has been the hallmark of this work, and its ongoing expansion, testimony to God's calling and anointing.

Pastor Andrew Edwards

Living Hope ministries: A God honouring ministry with a heart to change and renew lives.

Andrew Fadoju – Pastor of Worthing Elim Church

Contents

*Trust in the Lord with all your heart
and lean not on your own understanding;
in all your ways acknowledge him,
and he will make your paths straight.*
Proverbs 3 : 5-6 (NIV)

CHAPTER 1

Under Suspicion

The security guard's eyes narrowed. "Stop the car."
He had his hand up and he meant business.

My son, Jonathan, had just leaned out of the window and taken a photograph. Innocent enough, but he had chosen to take his picture outside a government building.

We were in Nigeria, West of Africa. Under the banner of *Living Hope Ministries*, we had spent several days ministering to the poor, we were returning to our hotel late at night. Nigeria is such a beautiful country but we had hardly seen anything of the place, so after lunch I suggested taking a walk.

"Richard," our host smiled indulgently, "it is far too hot."

True to the song by Noel Coward, Mad dogs, and Englishmen go out in the midday sun... I hadn't really thought about the heat but in the dry season, the daytime temperatures can soar as high as 40 degrees.

Sensing my disappointment, he smiled. "Tell you what, we will take you for a drive."

As soon as we were underway, we began to relax and enjoy the tree-lined avenues and stunning buildings which make up this fabulous city. Jonni was itching to capture the moment.

"Is it all right to take photographs?" I asked.

"Fine," came the reply.

But clearly, by the look on the security guard's face, it wasn't.

We were taken to some sort of police station and I could see at once that we were in a very tricky situation. As soon as we got there, the camera was confiscated. The picture itself was probably of no consequence but as the security guards clustered around, we found ourselves under suspicion. Two of them seemed to be 'on our side' while others seemed to be determined to make the whole thing a real issue. We were protected to some degree because of the language barrier but I was alarmed when the word 'terrorist' was bandied about.

In situations like this, you are very much at the mercy of those around you. I recalled horror stories of people being held without charge in other countries for weeks and weeks, unable to get consular help, and 'lost' to their relatives on the outside. For me, what made matters worse was the fact that my son was with me. In the circumstances there was only one thing to do. We prayed.

After about two hours, it was decided that Jonni and I could leave, but to our dismay, they still held the Pastor. Our driver took us back to the hotel. At midnight we got the news that he had been released and would see us in church on Sunday. What a relief! However, when we all met on the Sunday, we discovered that the matter was far from over. We had to present ourselves at the police station for further investigation on Monday morning.

Dear Lord... what were we going to do now? The situation was escalating and there was no telling where it would all end.

This was a far cry from Fakenham where it all began...

CHAPTER 2

The Early Years

Time hasn't exactly stood still in Fakenham but it has certainly moved very slowly. Fakenham is in Norfolk, England and according to the 2001 census it has less than 8,000 souls. A market town with a cluster of traditional shops the name comes from a Saxon word meaning fair place or a place on a fair river. A far cry from a town guide in the late 1990s which named it the most boring place on earth. I was born and grew up there.

I was the first-born of two brothers. My birthday was in November 1949, a year when petrol went up to 2/3d (111/2p) a gallon, Billy Graham preached in Los Angeles in the 'Canvas Cathedral' (at that time the largest tent ever erected which could seat 6500 people) and Prince Charles had just had his first birthday.

Before she was married to my father, my mother, Kathleen May Barber, worked in the printing works. Printing was quite big in Norfolk. In 1862 Thomas Miller began a business which went on to attract the cream of London publishers.

My father, Reginald James Brunton, began work as a bricklayer, becoming a foreman and then a foreman supervisor towards the end of his working life. When I came along, they had been married for two years.

As a child, I developed a passion for sport. My brother Michael remembers my determination and dedication in everything I did. At school, I ran in the 220 yards (200

The Brunton Brothers

metres) race one sports day and by sheer determination I not only
got to the tape first, but so great was my joy that I leapt through it.

Football still brings out that competitive streak in me and the
passion has never left me. An avid supporter of Norwich City, we've

Determined as ever!

never really hit the big time,
but it's not through lack of
encouragement on my part!
I can get very worked up, but
my language has always made
people laugh. No, I don't
swear, never have, but you
may well find me rushing
down the terraces and telling
whoever it is, "not to do such
a naughty thing again!"

In the late 50s, early 60s, people were not so perturbed about
children being left to their own devices so Michael and I enjoyed
the countryside around us. When I was taking part in the Duke
of Edinburgh Award (Bronze), we used to go camping and I
remember one occasion when I got up to make my breakfast.
I decided that as the weather wasn't so great, I'd move the stove
into the tent. Unfortunately, a gust of wind blew the stove over and
the tent caught fire. In the ensuing panic, I lost the tent and my
sleeping bag, but thank goodness, I was able to save what really
mattered... my breakfast! Even as I relate these seemingly
innocuous incidents in my life I can see the Lord's hand at work.
I enjoy the challenge of the race, I have never lost my passion for
the gospel and even in the midst of trouble, there is always
something positive to hold on to.

When I became a Christian, my father and I used to have
terrible arguments. He had lost his mother when he was only seven
years old and he never really came to terms with his loss.

My father was in India during the Second World War and at
the time, the British were absolutely paranoid that the Japanese

were going to break through their lines. Everyone had heard that they were ruthless and merciless people. My father never lost the memory and he carried that fear most of his life. As a small boy, I remember him being plagued with nightmares, waking up in the dead of night shouting, "The Japs are coming, the Japs are coming…"

My father was an incredibly clever man. He could mend or fix anything but he had little patience with anybody trying to learn how to do the same thing. I have never been particularly practical so if my bike got a puncture my Dad would become extremely angry at my feeble attempts to sort it out myself. I know now that he never meant it but his attitude would always leave me feeling utterly useless. As a result I grew up believing that 'my Dad can do absolutely everything but I can do nothing.'

Dad in the centre

As an adult, I now realise that he was probably very tired after a long day's work. It takes time and patience to explain things to a small boy and all he wanted to do was rest. Understandable as that is, the sad thing is that his irritation compounded my own feelings of inadequacy.

Even today if I can't fathom out something and my boys muscle in as if to take over, I say, "Don't do it for me, show me how to do it."

I don't know if my father ever came to the Lord. He died in October 2002 and although I have peace about him, I have to leave him with the Lord. However, on a personal level, he was always encouraging of me and followed my progress with a great deal of interest. Early years were challenging but Dad's love for us and the family was great, he would have been so proud of his grandsons if he saw them today..

The odd thing is, both my mother and Elaine's mother started going to church soon after both our Dads died. I often wonder whether the women of their generation who wanted to love the Lord, and to follow Him, denied themselves the opportunity for the sake of peace in the home. So many of their men folk would have been damaged by the war, that it seemed but a small sacrifice to keep their own desires to themselves.

I first became interested in church when a boy called Richard Warnes invited me to the afternoon Baptist Sunday School. Strangely enough, Richard himself wasn't a Christian so I am not sure why he invited me, but as things turned out, I am very glad that he did! Six months later I went to a rally led by Bill Batham, an American evangelist in the 1960s. This was my defining moment. Everything suddenly made absolute sense, and I became a Christian. My brother Michael made a profession of faith soon after me.

In primary school, I had had a fairly bad time with bullying. I'm not sure why the other boys picked on me, possibly for no particular reason other than it was my turn. I was a bit of a loner and I didn't have lots of close friends. My brother, although younger than me, was far more outgoing and had quite a gang of friends. When I surrendered my life to Jesus, the remarkable thing is, all the bullying stopped.

By the time I was thirteen years old, a couple called Mike and Diane Brown, with a teacher called Mary Usher, used to pray for some of the young people coming along to the meetings at the church. I think those prayers had a significant impact on my life. Almost as soon as I got saved, I began to preach. For the first time ever, I felt I was doing something positive.

Once a fishing village, Overstrand on the North Norfolk coast has become a quiet place noted for its neat bungalows and carefully manicured gardens. The village was made popular by the writer Clement Scott, who included it in his romantic tales of the area. Scott renamed it Poppyland, because of the many wild red poppies which grew in the grass and wheat fields along the hedgerows and on the cliffs. It's a beautiful place to be but for me the memories of staying in Overstrand have a greater significance. As a young man I went to conferences with the Baptist Church and at one of those conferences someone prophesied over me.

"God's got a big work for you. A very big work."

Although I was very young at the time, I carried that word in my heart for many years. I knew that if God said it, He would do it. I've never been one to spend a lot of time trying to make prophecy work, nor do I speculate about it, but I do remember these things and later on, as I look back I can see the hand of God at work. It's only as I write these words that I can see the full extent of His plan.

My parents were totally baffled by my conversion. My brother Michael 'did church' for a while but then he drifted back into living his life the way he'd always lived. I think my father thought that was normal. It was as if Michael had done the religion thing and got over it. It was just a phase of life. But for me, it was something more. I was still doing it.

Years later, after I met Elaine and took her home, she shared her testimony. I was amazed to see my father listening avidly. I think he understood for the first time that I wasn't a crackpot and that others believed the same as I did, but I have no idea if he had made his own personal peace with God.

The preaching came about because the Baptist Church used to hold open-air services. Looking back, I suppose it was fairly unusual but we used to go around all the Norfolk villages. One night, Max Dixon, who was heading all this up, turned to the small crowd gathered to listen to us and said, "And now young Richard Brunton will give his testimony." I gulped. That was the first I'd heard about it. I had no time to think about what I should say before the microphone was in my hand and I was on!

Later, Kathleen Harrison, a local preacher, used to take me to the Railways Mission in Melton Constable. I was discovering that

God had a work for me to do and, although in so many areas I felt lacking and inadequate, I was joyfully discovering that God had a purpose for my life, and a work for me to do.

At first I led the service and she preached but one day the people said they would like to hear me preach. I was incredibly shy and people still find it hard to believe I do what I do, but the next time we went there, she took the service while I preached my first ever sermon. I preached on Daniel chapter 3 and I still have the notes to this day. Kathleen and her husband became my spiritual parents. I would pray with them and ask their advice, knowing this godly couple would give me wise counsel.

At seventeen, I sensed clearly God's call to full-time ministry, but it was to be 23 years later that the door opened for that. The Lord spoke about a big work in store that would involve speaking to crowds; but I never really took that in. While waiting, there were many doors of service, including spare and part-time pastoring. Although waiting for full-time ministry was difficult, I knew that God had called me and had impressed upon me, as a teenager, the scriptures from 1 Peter 5 and 2 Timothy 4.

It was about that time I had a dream. I had only just become a Christian and in the dream it was judgement time. Everyone was being brought before the Lord to give an account of his or her life. I was waiting and waiting for my turn. It's still very vivid in my mind. Then all at once the Lord said to me, "What have you got to say for yourself?"

I remember looking at the Lord. I don't remember what he looked like, but I knew it was Him because of the whole atmosphere of the place where I was. "Lord," I said, "I've got nothing to say for myself and there's nothing good in me but please accept me because Jesus died for me."

That dream has been like an anchor to me and I still use it when I talk to people. I knew even then that it's not about me. It's all about Him. I can do nothing to gain my salvation. Salvation comes only through faith in Christ.

I thought about going to Spurgeon's Bible College but after a lot of prayer, I felt that I was called to preach, but 'not yet' so I set out for teacher training college.

In 1960 I had taken my 11 + examination. The educational system at that time deemed that everyone who passed the 11+ went to grammar school, and from there to college and then on to University. Anyone who failed the 11+ was thought to have a more vocational aptitude in life. Pupils from secondary modern schools went on to be plumbers and shop girls. I was already at a disadvantage because I had failed my 11+, but I am of the opinion that if you work hard you can achieve your ambitions. When I came to the end of my secondary school days, I seized the day.

At that time in Norfolk, you could take an exam to go to King's Lynn Technical College where you could do 'O' levels and 'A' levels. I worked hard, passed the exam and set my sights on the 'O' and 'A' levels. Once I'd finished at the Tec, armed with the qualifications I needed, I went for an interview at Brighton to attend the College of Education.

I decided to teach Religious Education and I have to say that my interview was not an easy one. I reckon I was chosen because I was the only evangelical applying for the course. The-powers-that-be held the view that if you were a Bible believing Christian, that was just dumb. Believing the Bible was all right for teenagers but not for adults. I'm sure they planned to knock some sense into me. The attitude was, that a mature person would cease to have such naïve views.

After the interview, I knelt down outside the college and prayed, "Lord I never want to come back to this place unless this is where *You* want me to be."

Then the acceptance came.

The only friend I am still in touch with from my school days is Brian Nash. He used to go to the Salvation Army and is still involved in the church in Fakenham. My truly lasting friendships stem from those teacher-training days at the college in Brighton.

After a year, I was involved in the Christian Union and by 1970 I had became the president. Brighton Christian Union was quite well connected. We had some great preachers including Terry Virgo, (who later became the founder of the New Frontiers network of churches), Campbell McAlpine (a highly respected Bible teacher and author), and Denis Clark (a South African evangelist, who began by working with Youth for Christ before establishing the prayer group, Intercessors for Britain).

Part of my duties was to help set up a meeting for new students. We put on a Freshers' Squash meeting and a man called Nigel Goodwin who had been in the TV series Z Cars came. At the end of the meeting, we gave an invitation for anyone to come to Christ. Several people accepted the invitation and as president of the union it was my job to follow them up. Elaine was one of those new converts. Her friend Delyse, who had just lost her father, later gave her life to Christ as well.

"The river of God will lead you in many ways and I see you going through three doors," Trisha McCarthy, a friend from college prophesied. "One door is the door of suffering where you will see brokenness and you will see something of the suffering of the Lord and endure tribulation with his humility. The second door is glory. You'll be full of wonder, bowing down as you see His glory. The third door is one of fulfilment of service, a place of blessing, a place of inheritance. You'll see his power, weep with Him and the river of God will carry you through suffering to his glory and your heart will be glad."

Compared to some, my suffering has been minute, but having seen glimpses of the glory of God, and having a sense of fulfilment, as well as weeping when I've seen God doing things through me that I never thought possible or that I'd be a part of, I realise that this prophecy was very significant.

Although I was attracted to my wife Elaine almost straightaway, we didn't start dating until January 1971. I always felt I only wanted one romance. I'm a wholehearted person and I didn't want to start a relationship with just anyone. I had liked other girls but Elaine was my first and only serious girlfriend.

Elaine became a Christian within the first week of college. She could see the man who was speaking knew God in a close way. She had always been to Sunday school and she knew about God but she didn't have the same sort of close relationship.

After she had given her heart to the Lord, Elaine went to the Christian Union, and at that time I was the president. She was in the year below me but we became good friends. Eventually we had a meeting in the library to discuss whether or not we should go out together and after that meeting, we began dating.

Before I met Elaine, I remember having a tussle with the Lord as to whether or not I was willing to be single for Him. I was walking from the Steyne in Brighton to Percival Terrace, the place where I lodged. The distance is about a mile and I found myself praying with each step of the way. Almost at the point of arrival I had made a momentous choice. "Alright Lord," I said, "if it's what you really want for my life, I will be content to remain single." I had once again laid everything down before God. I hadn't taken that decision lightly. It was costly to me and I had no idea if God would take me at my word, but because of my deep love for Him I was willing to do anything he asked of me. In fact He didn't ask me to remain a single man, because now I had met Elaine and the rest, as they say, is history.

I was very clear in my mind as a young Christian that a sexual relationship is only acceptable within a committed marriage. As much as I loved Elaine and found her very attractive, it was important to honour those boundaries. I remember some years later being asked by someone in Pakistan "Was your marriage an arranged marriage or a love marriage? "

I believe my marriage to Elaine is both. It was a love marriage that had been planned by God. Courtship, a word little used these days, is all about respect and love. We both wanted, and still want the best for each other. Marriage is a covenant, which should not be based on intimacy alone, but be firmly based on the word of God. Seeking God and His will is very important. The scriptures encourage us to flee adultery and to exercise self-control. Of course, to live a godly life is best motivated by the desire to please Him. However, it is also important to be aware of the consequences of sinful behaviour. The consequences of an intimate relationship outside of marriage can reap a fearful result. Christians are urged to exercise self-control and be like Jesus. Jesus was tempted in every way and in every area as we are, yet He did not sin. He can help us to overcome the urge to do wrong things too. I loved Elaine with all my heart (I still do) but we waited for each other until after we were married. We made our vows to God before we slept together. Elaine was my only girlfriend.

I remember that when I was 14 or 15 years old and praying about my future, I read 2 Timothy 4 v 2 *Preach the word! Be ready in season and out of season*. 1 had also read the whole of 1 Peter 5. I was going down to preach in Churchill Square and someone came running up to me and pushed a piece of paper into my hand. It was from Elaine. She had only been a Christian a few weeks and had been praying for me and the Lord had given her 2 Timothy 4. That certainly sent my pulses racing.

I think I am a romantic because I can take anyone to the very spot where I asked Elaine to marry me. We walked from her

Elaine and I at Brighton Teacher Training College

lodgings at Falmer and we came to some steps. I knew this was the moment. I asked her and then before she could answer I went on to say, "If you do marry me, you need to know that I am going to be in full-time ministry and it is going to be hard."

I'm glad I said it. Elaine told me at once that it didn't

matter. I think we should be open and honest with people especially when making big decisions in life. All too often I have come across men in full-time ministry, and their wives never realised what being the wife of a minister would entail. It is a huge challenge having to share your spouse with everybody and can all to easily create serious problems in a marriage.

I had opened my heart, and I was waiting for my answer. Imagine my joy when Elaine said, "Yes."

One day Elaine asked me to pray for her. She said she couldn't say why but I prayed. Later on, I discovered that she was concerned because she wasn't having a menstrual cycle. In fact she'd never had a proper cycle. I prayed, and God answered our prayers, which meant that when we were married, our first son, Paul came along. After his birth, Elaine's cycle stopped again so we prayed again. It turned out that we had to pray each time we wanted a baby. When I look back on God's blessing, I am amazed. We now have five sons!

Psalm 127 v 3-5 *Behold, children are a heritage from the LORD, the fruit of the womb is a reward. Like arrows in the hand of a warrior, so are the children of one's youth. Happy is the man who has his quiver full of them.* (NIV)

That experience is what gives me the faith to pray for couples in Kenya, Romania (and even here in the UK) who are childless and long for a family. God has answered our prayers over and over. At Woodingdean Baptist Church a grandfather came up to me to thank me for praying for his daughter. She had had a child and he was so thrilled with his grandson! And many years later when I was in Kisumu, Kenya, I gave a call for people to come forward if they wanted prayer. Among them were women who had been unable to have children. When a woman is unable to have children in Western society it is heartbreaking, but in African culture it can be devastating. Much of a woman's worth is still bound up in her ability to have children, especially sons.

I prayed for these ladies and a year later, when my son Philip went to the same place, a man came over to him with a baby in his arms. He beamed at Philip, pointed to the baby and said, "This is Richard Brunton."

My time at the teacher training college in Brighton became a learning ground for many other things besides the classroom. In the area of deliverance I was extremely naïve and very inexperienced. A good friend had met a young man in the town and had brought him back to the college. He wasn't a Christian and was in fact, quite disturbed. I was talking with them both one night when he became very hostile and upset. Indeed, I could see that we were in danger. He was over six foot and a well-built man and appeared as if he was about to fly into an uncontrollable rage. The situation was serious, but the lady was kneeling in prayer, apparently oblivious to what was going on.

I heard what I later realized was a demonic voice which sounded nothing like the man who is now a dear friend. "You are safe," it said, "but he is mine." At that moment, he moved towards me in a very menacing way and for a second the whole of my life flashed before me. I wondered if I would ever get to marry Elaine or even if I would see her again! With not too much faith and certainly with no experience, I pointed my finger straight at him and said, "In the Name of Jesus, stop!" And to my utter relief, he did. That gave me courage to say," In the Name of Jesus, lay down." As he went to the bed and lay down, I grabbed hold of the lady's hand and ran from the room.

This story was a real learning curve for me. A mixture of seeing something of the power of Jesus and my own dependency on Him and also how much I had to learn. It taught me that spiritual warfare is very real. I hadn't had an experience like the sons of Sceva which was a mercy, but I realised the seriousness of it. What little of the power of Christ I was moving in, I knew enough to get us out of that situation, but I realised that I needed to grow. It was imperative that I should not only be able to get out of such situations but be able to deliver someone from the grip of the enemy.

Acts 19 v. 13 - 16 *Some Jews who went around driving out evil spirits tried to invoke the name of the Lord Jesus over those who were demon-possessed. They would say, "In the name of Jesus, whom Paul preaches, I command you to come out." Seven sons of Sceva, a Jewish chief priest, were doing this. (One day) the evil spirit answered them, "Jesus I know, and I know about Paul, but who are you?" Then the man who had the evil spirit jumped on them and overpowered them all. He gave them such a beating that they ran out of the house naked and bleeding.*

I feel in some ways I failed the man who is now my friend by my inexperience but I thank God he did eventually get set free. He later met some more experienced Christians and is completely changed from the man he was in those days. The devil has no right over anyone who comes under the Lordship of Christ. Those who *"the Son sets free are free indeed."* John 8 v. 36. This gentle giant of a man went on to marry the lady mentioned earlier and we have remained friends for a great many years. His life has wonderfully changed and I learnt some very important lessons.

After being engaged for about a year, Elaine and I got married on October 27th 1973. It was the happiest day of my life. We had waited for Elaine to finish her training and we were both fixed up with jobs. Elaine had a post as a primary school teacher at Ashurstwood near East Grinstead and I was already working in the same area. We were to live at Sharpthorne and shortly after we moved there I was asked to be pastor at neighbouring West Hoathly.

West Hoathly days

For our wedding service we chose two hymns. *To God be the Glory* and *When we walk with the Lord.* These hymns had a big impact on our lives right from the start of our marriage. One line from *When we walk with the Lord,* says: *What He says we will do, where He sends we will go; never fear only trust and obey.*

As I look back, I realise that as we made those words a prayer, God heard us.

There are still times when He reminds me of what we promised.

The minister, Peter Hetherington preached on Proverbs 3 v 5 & 6. *Trust in the LORD with all thine heart; and lean not unto thine own understanding. In all thy ways acknowledge him, and he shall direct thy paths.*

The registrar, Mr Heddle, was a very old man. When we came out to sign the register he murmured, "Trust in the LORD with all thine heart." After our honeymoon, we went back to church and I said, "Why did you say that verse? Was it just because you remembered what the Pastor preached?"

"Oh no," he said. "I didn't hear what Peter preached. I was praying for you that morning and the Lord gave me that verse."

When we walk with the Lord in the light of His Word,
What a glory He sheds on our way!
While we do His good will, He abides with us still,
And with all who will trust and obey.
Trust and obey, for there's no other way
To be happy in Jesus, but to trust and obey.
Not a shadow can rise, not a cloud in the skies,
But His smile quickly drives it away;
Not a doubt or a fear, not a sigh or a tear,
Can abide while we trust and obey.
Trust and obey, for there's no other way
To be happy in Jesus, but to trust and obey.
Not a burden we bear, not a sorrow we share,
But our toil He doth richly repay;
Not a grief or a loss, not a frown or a cross,

But is blessed if we trust and obey.
Trust and obey, for there's no other way
To be happy in Jesus, but to trust and obey.
But we never can prove the delights of His love
Until all on the altar we lay;
For the favour He shows, for the joy He bestows,
Are for them who will trust and obey.
Trust and obey, for there's no other way
To be happy in Jesus, but to trust and obey.
Then in fellowship sweet we will sit at His feet.
Or we'll walk by His side in the way.
What He says we will do, where He sends we will go;
Never fear, only trust and obey.
Trust and obey, for there's no other way
To be happy in Jesus, but to trust and obey.
Text: John H. Sammis, 1846-1919
Music: Daniel B. Towner, 1850-1919

Some have remarked that when I talk about *Living Hope Ministries* I always use the 'royal we'. This whole ministry has always been the ministry of both Elaine and myself. She may not have always come on trips with me, especially in the early years when we were bringing up our five boys, Paul, born in 1975, Philip born in 1979, Matthew who came along in 1982, Stephen who was born in 1984 and last but not least, Jonathan born in 1988, but she has always been a vital part of what I do.

The door through which I entered full-time ministry was to prove a great challenge, and it was totally unexpected when the Lord took me to Africa in November 1994. He told me He was to do a "new thing". This "new thing", I discovered, would be working with many churches in the UK rather than pastoring a church. This would initially support ministry in Kenya, Uganda, Tanzania and Rwanda, Spain, New Jersey and Chicago. It involves writing to hundreds of pastors and leaders and making television programmes and radio programmes. Now the ministry is in over twenty countries and is still growing!

Much as I rely on the Lord and give all the glory to Him, how could I have managed without Elaine's wise counsel, her prayers, her unselfish love and her encouragement?

CHAPTER 3

Dugouts and Mountains

Elaine and I settled happily into married life and our
dearest friends, Delyse and John Oxford joined us at West
Hoathly Evangelical Church. West Hoathly itself is a
picturesque village situated on the edge of the Ashdown
Forest. Its only claim to fame is the site for a warning beacon
on Finch Field, and the Bluebell Railway, but we were happy
there.

Delyse became my secretary and when we all went to West
Hoathly Evangelical Church, she helped me to write the church
magazine. We have kept up our friendship even though they now
live in New Zealand.

The four of us still have a running joke from those days.
John had a little red Mini and coming up to a junction John
asked, "Is it all right to go?"

"It's all right...," Delyse said anxiously watching another
car approaching the same junction, "if you're quick." How quick
was always the question!

Although it was a small fellowship, being the Pastor of
West Hoathly chapel, a full-time schoolteacher and with Elaine
in a full-time teaching post, it proved to be too much. Elaine
decided to give up her job to fully support me and soon after, our
first son Paul came along.

In the 1980s, Terry Virgo, who was born and raised in
Brighton, started a small church movement which has since
grown into an international group of churches in 29 nations.
He called it New Frontiers. I wrote to Terry to tell him that
since the age of 17 I had the call on my life to preach and thus
our two paths converged.

West Hoathly Evangelical Free Church
Chapel Row, West Hoathly

Dear Terry,

I have been feeling for some time the need for covering and direction in the local church setting.

I have excellent links and fellowship with David Dominy but I still feel the need for particular apostolic-like input. I don't think I want to use jargon but I do want us to really move on in the Lord. I feel the Lord's hand is on the relationship which had its beginnings in college days with both yourself and David Fellingham.

We are a small fellowship covering about 30 people. Just over one third are baptised in the Spirit and only a handful are directly wary about the things of the Holy Spirit. I feel the majority of the fellowship would accept you taking an apostolic role though many would be cautious at first. I have mooted the suggestion of someone coming in but am seeking to be wise.

The Anglican church in the village has come alive recently and there are baptised in the Spirit believers. This is good but I am concerned to know just where and how God is wanting to build his kingdom here.

Would you please pray for us and respond as God leads? You are welcome to preach almost any Sunday in November or December or I could come over to you to discuss things further. There is a great deal of potential here and I do desire to see it all harnessed to God's glory. David Dominy is aware of our situation as to some extent is David Fellingham.

The Lord bless you
Your brother Richard.

After that, I used to go to a prayer meeting with the founders of New Frontiers. Eventually Terry agreed to come and preach at West Hoathly. It was during one of his visits that he exhorted us to think more deeply about what we were going to do with our lives. Also I shared the morning office with a good friend and squash partner Rev. Michael Allen. We met on Fridays and one morning a passage from Exodus spoke powerfully about moving on with God and being confident He would presence Himself with us. As a result of that, we were drawn to Clarendon Church Brighton where eventually I did a year's Bible College.

In 1992, I went out to Malaysia with Steve Walford, one of the Pastors at Clarendon. Despite many changes over the years, we have remained firm friends, and in fact on my 60th birthday, he came to join in the surprise party celebrations.

1992 was the time when revival was taking place and the general consensus of opinion was that Christians should go to such places and get a taste of what God was doing. It was also a season when Pastors were being offered sabbaticals. After talking to Rodney Kingston (a well respected Christian leader in Worthing), Steve decided to go to Sarawak and I went with him. Sarawak is one of two Malaysian states on the island of Borneo. Affectionately known as the Land of the Hornbills, (the national bird) Sarawak was officially granted independence in 1963 and became part of the Federation of Malaysia the same year.

Coming into Kuala Lumpur we stayed with a brother who was commuting from Australia. He was reasonably happy about it but having just landed I was missing Elaine already!

Clearly, back then, the tourist trail was not quite so sophisticated but look on any Internet website now and you will see that Sarawak is a land of vast primeval rainforests, national parks, and awe-inspiring limestone caves. It is home to the largest caves in the world, and the longest underground cavity cave known to man. In other parts of the world, deforestation has wreaked havoc but in Sarawak, the forests are still so dense that rivers form the backbone of the transportation system.

We flew on to Kuching where we met Mun Heng. It is essential to have a good guide, one who knows the river, can speak the language and knows the people. Mun Heng was just such a man, and he was particularly keen for us to meet with tribal groups not normally reached by missionaries or tourists.

Kuching Evangelical Church

We began what turned out to be a four-hour journey by road, to take us to the river, which would, in turn, take us to the Iban tribe. These people were once the dreaded head hunters of Borneo. Just to encourage us a little further, we were told that the river was home to a crocodile, which had just eaten a child, and that it was not uncommon to see a python taking a swim. All at once, I didn't feel very brave. For us a python spelled danger but for the indigenous people, a python meant food.

The heat was oppressive, the river a brackish brown/green colour, but I did my best to enjoy the trip. However, being in a canoe with twenty people and all their luggage when it was only designed for ten, was challenging to say the least. I've been teased about it since, but probably my insistence on wearing a shirt and tie on all occasions may not have been very practical either, but I never lost my passion to share the gospel with the people.

The longhouse was on stilts, which keeps it above the jungle. We climbed a steep muddy bank and walked along a rush pathway to get there. Inside there was a long corridor with rooms leading off. Eleven families lived in the one house.

The men were covered with tattoos on their arms and legs and as we came in, each family offered us a drink. I wasn't too sure what we were being offered but it would have been rude or churlish not to take it.

The Iban tribes-people have a delicacy called the sago worm which they enjoy. To get it they fell a palm and leave it to rot for several months. A beetle lays its eggs inside and when it hatches the sago worm, a kind of maggot, emerges. It is as big as a man's thumb and a creamy yellow in colour. Because it is high in protein, the people eat it raw or deep-fried. Thankfully, I was not offered any of them!

In this day and age, visitors to that part of the world, have the opportunity to take jungle treks when they spend the night in an Iban tribal longhouse. The locals are used to entertaining tourists, even taking them out on a hunting trip. Steve Walford and I had come, at their invitation, with the express purpose of sharing the gospel with these people.

Some would criticise Christians for taking the gospel to far-flung places. They hate the idea of their culture being altered and yet if no one had told these people about Jesus, they would still be practising their head-hunting. It's all very well handling the relics the tourists flock to see, but one can so easily forget the fear and bondage such practices brought with them. It was a hard tradition to stamp out because the tribesmen believed that by drinking the blood of their victims they gained spiritual powers. We were glad to tell them that Jesus gives His Spirit freely to those who put their trust in Him.

After spending some time with them, we moved on to the second longhouse. Along the river, the foliage comes down to the water's edge but every now and then there is a muddy patch, which serves as a landing stage. We came across the occasional man with a long pole working his way upriver in a dugout canoe and in other places we saw people bathing in the waters. Every now and them, the jungle is so dense the trees formed a tunnel over the water, cutting out the light and making it shadowy even in the middle of the day.

There are, in fact, thousands of longhouses in Sarawak and these days they are part of the cultural eco tour trail. Having said that, the second longhouse was much more primitive than the first. I was already struggling with the heat and lack of sleep. Night time had been punctuated with the sound of dogs barking (they lazed around the longhouse all day) and the cockerels gave us such an early morning call that I was pretty shattered.

When we arrived the people put on a ritual dance. Their costumes were very colourful and they wore high-feathered headbands and tabards with tassels. They danced in a rhythmical

Pastor Johnnny in Sarawak

way around long poles which were snapped together while the musicians played drums and bells. It was all done with great speed and skill as the audience clapped and whooped with joy. I wondered how many bruised ankles the dancers had suffered before they got it right. After a while, they invited us to join in and although it was not something I was keen to do, I made a valiant effort. Once again we shared the Word of God as the people sat cross-legged on the floor and listened with rapt attention.

Then much to my dismay, there was talk of going to a third longhouse. Even though Sarawak is considered to be one of the hidden paradises of Borneo I had quite frankly had enough. I was ready to go home and in my prayers I complained to the Lord.

However, the Headman of the third longhouse was more than willing for our party to go and share Jesus with his family, and so off we went. It was further down the river, much more remote than the first two longhouses and if I'd thought the first two were primitive the third was even more so. We discovered that we were the first white men the people had ever seen. It was very humbling because they wanted us to have the best chair etc and we were treated like royalty.

I was given the privilege of preaching the first and only Gospel they had ever heard. I loved every minute but of course seeing the expressions on their faces, I felt a bit guilty that I hadn't wanted to go. I felt even more guilty when twenty out of thirty people present wanted to give their lives to Christ! The next day we encouraged them to take down the fetishes devoted to witchcraft and demons. Although I have no idea as to their value, when they went out into the jungle to burn it all, I felt like I'd seen a re-enactment of the Ephesians church in Acts when they burned their occultish paraphernalia.

Acts 19 v. 19 *A number who had practised sorcery brought their scrolls together and burned them publicly. When they calculated the value of the scrolls, the total came to fifty thousand drachmas.*

We returned to Kuala Lumpur and from there we went to Korea. Steve and I explored the city until one day we got a bit lost. The one thing that sticks out about Seoul was when we unwittingly walked through the exit of a House of Horror. What began as gruesome gradually became less and less frightening until we emerged at the entrance where we were confronted by an extremely angry ticket collector!

While we were in Korea, we made our way to Yoido Full Gospel Church, founded by David Yonggi Cho and his mother-in-law, Choi Ja-shil, both Assemblies of God pastors. The church had experienced phenomenal growth. What had begun with just six people, including one old woman who only came in to get out of the rain, had become a massive church. In 1973, the new 10,000 seat auditorium was completed and in the same year Prayer Mountain, a sanctuary where individuals can lock themselves away in small cubicles or grottos for prayer and fasting, was established. Before long Prayer Mountain was being visited by more than a million people each year, myself included. Despite the expansion of the auditorium to seat 12,000 in 1983, even seven Sunday services were insufficient to accommodate the entire membership. Church membership reached 400,000 in 1984, and by the time I went there in 1992, it was closer to 700,000. In 2010 the church had more than 830,000 members.

It was amazing to take part in one of the all-night prayer meetings which are held on a regular basis. There were thousands of people. The auditorium seated 45,000, and I still carry the image of those young Koreans, all desperate for God, crying their eyes out for their country as they prayed. When you see people praying with that level of intensity there is a temptation to feel that you'll never reach the mark in your own personal prayer life. Almost as soon as the thought entered my mind, the Lord said to me, "Be challenged but don't feel guilty."

One of the ways in which the Korean pastors deal with people who have problems is to send them to Prayer Mountain and tell them to wait until God gives them as answer. No counselling, no advice, no long sessions with the Pastor, just go to the mountain and seek God. It seems a good idea to me, although with our frenetic life style in the West, it would be almost impossible in this country.

I was away for about three weeks for what had turned out to be an amazing experience, but when I got back I had missed Elaine so dreadfully that I told her, "I'm never doing that again."

We both thought this would be a once in a lifetime trip, although in her heart of hearts Elaine always believed the Lord was whispering that I would be going abroad again. I am sure that was why, when some time later Africa was mentioned, Elaine was prepared and she encouraged me to go.

When I got back from Korea, little did I know that the Lord had a much bigger plan which was about to explode onto us, turning upside down our uneventful and comfortable life.

CHAPTER 4

New Beginnings

As New Frontiers grew, they wanted to plant a church in Lancing. As I have already mentioned, I had fellowshipped with Terry before. We both felt now was the right time for me to take up full-time ministry and so I was invited to head up the work.

We began with some preparatory meetings at Clarendon but I noticed that the attendance of the Lancing people themselves was often sparse. I think I was so excited about being asked to be in full-time leadership that it didn't really register at the time. The new church plant was called Grace Church and we met together in a school in Lancing. However, when wheels had turned a little further and we had had a meeting with Dave Fellingham and some of the Lancing leaders, Elaine and I came away deeply saddened. Although there was nothing personal against us, it was obvious that the people at Lancing would have preferred one of their own number to lead the new fellowship. They were hurt and upset and we were embarrassed.

When the church actually started, we could see that people were not too happy about the situation and although everyone did their best not to let it show, with such strong undercurrents already undermining the beginning of the work, it was a hard time.

Despite everything we went ahead and the church was planted. A few years later, some of those who had felt wrong-footed by the beginnings of the church had left but we had a reasonable number of people. Then the church began to attract some very needy people. That's just as it should be, but financially it put a strain on the work. Those who were able were giving very well but once I as a full-time minister, had been paid there was precious little left over for the rest of our needs.

Elaine sensed the unease with my appointment but she very much preferred to remain in the background and support me in prayer and service. There has been a great tendency to stereotype the role of a Pastor's wife but hosting coffee mornings and being up-front in ministry is not her way. It has been good over recent years for Elaine to find her own role rather than have one cast for her.

As time went on, I began to feel increasingly uncomfortable. I felt that the atmosphere was changing. New concepts of leadership were heralded and I didn't fit the bill.

At about the same time, I remember a leaders' prayer meeting in Brighton, where someone had a picture of a lot of broken glass. In the picture, I had been given the unenviable task of clearing up a mess which was not of my making. This picture was followed the next Sunday by an amazing prophecy about me getting a real breakthrough and my ministry growing. A few days later however I received a visit from a leading brother. He said that I should lay down full-time ministry and go back to teaching! What a contrast!

After much prayer I wrote to the brothers concerned a letter. Here are some extracts:

"I have weaknesses but you must know that for me to write this causes me much concern. I only want to know the will of God for my family, Grace Church and the Kingdom's sake. I am not being awkward. We have shown in the past a willingness to respond to apostolic authority. We left a ministry in West Hoathly and potentially rendered ourselves homeless in doing so.

I gave up my teaching career of 17 years and after a very long house-moving process, came to Lancing. We were delighted to take up full-time ministry but found it very hard to leave Brighton and the Coldean/Patcham area where we were greatly loved and respected.

Lancing proved to be very different and the last five years have taken a considerable toll on us as a family. Our hope though has been that God has called me and that we were here through Apostolic direction and the backing of Clarendon eldership.

Prophetic words are also a great comfort and I include some of them.

Brothers, I must know that the current thinking is of God. We have been obedient but I dare not put my family through any more trauma unless it is abundantly clear God is speaking.

What was shared about going back to work and not being a number one, was not accompanied by a prophetic word, word of knowledge or scripture. However the previous Sunday a prophetic word by a respected leader was brought, saying that God was going to roll away the reproach of the years and was going to give me a new dimension of authority in my ministry and that I was to be confident of moving ahead, unafraid of men's faces and to trust confidently in God's call. This Pastor knows very little of my situation in Lancing.

Recently when praying for Lancing at a Sussex Pastors' gathering, two pictures were brought. One was of me in a boat. I had been rowing as if through reeds but one more push and the church would be clear. The other was of me picking up debris from a storm-stricken house, a thankless task, but clearing to rebuild.

It was prophesied in 1992 that God had called me to pastor the flock and to gently lead them. At the laying-on of hands for eldership, there were prophesies about me moving in authority as the pastor of the church.

In conclusion.

1. The gifts and calling of God are irrevocable. My gifts and calling were recognised by the Clarendon elders. Romans 11 v. 29

2. I believe scripture supports that a shepherd is accountable for his sheep regardless of how good a shepherd he is. Timothy at Ephesus needed Paul's support. He was timid and had a weak stomach, needed encouragement but God used him and built his church. I am the father of five boys and it could be argued that I have a lot to learn about fathering. It would be pretty drastic to take them away from me or me from them. As the current leader of Grace church, I have heaps to learn and welcome all attempts to make me a good shepherd to the flock but like my boys, I cannot disown them or hand them over unless God clearly tells me. I was made accountable to Him when I received the laying on of hands.

I recognise that God moves leaders around but I cannot move out of the position vested upon me by the laying on of hands unless it is in line with the word of God.

3. By the grace of God there has been fruit. Having lost about 26 people through difficult and recognised circumstances, we have gained 30, many of whom are new Christians. We are now 55 adults but could have been 23 unless God had been with us.

God has been working in marriages.

The outreach in the area has been considerable and we have enjoyed much of the present move of the Spirit.

Financially we have challenges but covenanting has more than doubled, with a number of people responding to the need to pay me.

I urge you to consider what I have shared and then to allow me to continue serving God's people on a salary relevant to our current situation.

Please give me the opportunity to attend some elders meetings and provide me with more leadership training. If someone could be seconded to come alongside, like Henry Tyler used to do, that would be a blessing. I truly want to do God's will and would like you to pray and think again. I purposely add that this letter comes from Elaine as well as myself. She has felt the pressures and is totally with me in what's written.

To add to the confusion, as I sent that letter, someone else gave me a prophecy. Sometimes, I used to preach in a church in Bildeston. The pastor at that time was a man called Bryan Land and when he heard of the changes we were experiencing, he contacted me with a word of encouragement. "Richard," he said, "God hasn't made you redundant."

As I waited for the brothers' response, I felt as if my whole life was on hold. I was aware of my calling and eager to follow the Lord but I also had the responsibility of providing for a wife and five small boys. I realised that we weren't a rich church and I was being paid a good salary for that time (1995). That was why I offered to take a cut in my wage, but eventually even that was deemed unacceptable.

Even after all that had been said, I didn't feel that leaving full-time ministry was the will of God for me. I made it clear time and again by saying, "I don't have any peace about this."

In the end, a meeting was set up in the August to inform the church that I would be stepping down from full- time ministry. Just before that church meeting I was taken to a house to see someone representing the wider movement and was told not to go back to the church for three months. I was encouraged to use the time to visit other churches and at the end of this time I could decide whether to come back to the Church as an unpaid Elder or leave altogether.

I was totally shattered. I drove back home to pick up Elaine, and was reduced to telling her what had happened in a few garbled sentences in the car on the way to the church meeting. At 44, at just one stroke, it was all gone. The ministry, my livelihood… everything.

I called Simon Iheancho of Freedom Embassy Ministries International in London and he was very encouraging. "God hasn't finished with you yet," he said. "You know, Richard, I feel the Lord is telling you to go to Kenya."

Kenya! That was a big step. I prayed about it long and hard. I only had a month's redundancy money, so there was no way I could risk that on an airfare - and for what? Some of my friends were a bit bemused by what I was saying but as I prayed about Simon's words, something struck a chord in my heart. I could feel the beginnings of a call. Elaine backed me 100%, but if I were going to go, the Lord would have to provide the money. I didn't want to risk using any of my redundancy money for the airfare. That was bread and butter for my children.

It was difficult to deal with all this and keep our spirits sweet at the same time. Elaine spent a lot of time praying about the situation and comforting me but we were also concerned about our boys, especially Paul. At seventeen, he was the oldest. He was very angry and because of his fierce loyalty towards us, he hated to see us hurt.

One couple prayed about helping me and felt they wanted to give me £100. They said, "Lord we're willing but we don't have £100." As they were praying, they heard the letterbox rattle. Amazingly, on the mat they found an envelope containing £100, so without further ado, they put it into another envelope and gave it to me!

As soon as I had enough money, Simon purchased the ticket and I went up to Heathrow. This was long before 9/11 and air travel was much more casual than it is now.

It had been arranged that I should meet Simon Iheancho, who was actually collecting the ticket for me. I waited and waited but there was no sign of him. Eventually, just as they were closing the departure gates, Simon rushed up saying, "I'm really sorry, Richard but I can't go today. We'll go tomorrow."

My heart sank. I'd prepared myself for this momentous adventure and now I had to go back to Lancing. The boys were a bit bemused to see me that night because we had made such a great deal of saying goodbye earlier that day, and here I was back again!

I set off the next night and I checked in. Again, no sign of Simon. Eventually his wife came up to me and gave me Simon's apologies. Once again, he was unable to go.

"But there's nothing to stop you, Richard," she said pushing a piece of paper in my hand. "You must go."

I gulped. What, on my own?

All I had was one name, Edward Tambo, and a telephone number and if that wasn't scary enough, I had no idea how to work the telephones in Kenya.

"Well, Lord," I said, "it's over to you."

Edward Tambo (far right)

This was just after the Rwandan genocide (1994) and as I waited in the departure lounge I met a Rwandan bishop. As we talked, although my situation was nowhere near as bad as his, I could certainly identify with him. He was unable to go back to his country and I too, felt like a refugee. I wasn't wanted back home and I was very conscious of the October deadline when I'd have to tell the people of Grace Church if I was coming back as an unpaid Elder or moving on to somewhere else.

Kenya lies across the equator in east-central Africa. It borders Somalia to the east, Ethiopia to the north, Tanzania to the south, Uganda to the west, and Sudan to the northwest. The coastal city of Mombasa is on the Indian Ocean. In the north, the land is arid but the southwest corner is in the fertile Lake Victoria Basin; and a length of the eastern depression of the Great Rift Valley separates western highlands from those that rise from the lowland coastal strip.

Kenya was thrown into the national headlines when on 6th February, 1952, the young Princess Elizabeth and her husband, Prince Philip, who were staying in the Aberdare Treetop Hotel woke to the news that her father, King George VI, had died of cancer. Princess Elizabeth returned to the UK as Queen Elizabeth II.

From October 1952 to December 1959, Kenya was under a state of emergency because of the Mau Mau rebellion but eventually Jomo Kenyatta formed a government and Kenya became independent on December 12 1963.

When Kenyatta died (August 22 1978) Kenya ranked highly among African countries both in terms of political stability and economic growth, but I knew that in fact God's people in Kenya had suffered alongside their fellow countrymen for years. They had maintained the Gospel flame despite the difficulties, and I felt truly humbled as I travelled to meet them for the first time.

As I have already explained, air travel was a lot more relaxed back then, so much so, that people could request to see inside the cockpit. I thought I might as well make the most of the experience so I called the stewardess over.

"I should like to see the flight deck," I said.

"Of course," she said. "I'll ask the pilot. What is your name?"

"Pastor Richard Brunton," I said.

I'm not sure why I used my title. I think I may have been remembering Brian Land's prophecy, "God hasn't made you redundant…" but who knows? All I know is, that answer I gave that stewardess was to become enormously significant. I saw the pilot and the flight deck. Fascinating!

As the aeroplane came in to land, the air stewardess picked me out. "I know you are a Pastor," she said. "It would be great if you would preach in my church." I could hardly believe my ears but she gave me her telephone number and invited me to ring. She must have had a conversation with her colleague on the plane.

The upshot of it was I spoke to her Pastor Bishop Arthur Gatonga and a few days later, Pastor Yonna his assistant invited me to preach in City Hall, an auditorium which could seat 2,000 people! I rang Elaine. "Please pray. This is all so bewildering. I'm really nervous."

But as I came away from the phone, (this was in the days before the mobile phone) I met Pastor Yonnah.

"Oh Richard," he said matter-of-factly, "you won't be preaching in City Hall tomorrow."

My heart sank. I'd only just told Elaine I was going to. Disappointed, I said, "Oh."

"Gatonga thinks you need a bigger setting," Yonnah went on. "He wants to see you."

A bigger setting? My mind was in a whirl as I hurried to meet him.

"I've heard very good things about you, brother," Gatonga said. "I want you to go over to Huruma."

Puzzled, I said, "What's at Huruma?"

"It's a 6,000 seater tent."

What! I was totally staggered. On my way over to Kenya, I was a washed-up preacher nobody wanted now I was on my way to preach in a vast tent!

In the morning I was in a small church with 20-30 people; in the afternoon in another church about the same size, and in the evening, the tent. The pastors who were with me in the morning, were aware that I was feeling nervous so they walked with me into the tent. It looked fairly full and I would hazard a guess that there were about 1400 waiting there. The atmosphere was electric and I was conscious of the dust rising over their heads as they worshipped the Lord. The women made a loud whooping noise which was a bit intimidating.

When I stood to preach, it was as if I'd always preached in that kind of setting, and afterwards so many people came forward for prayer. I remembered that back home when a lot of people come forward for prayer, especially for healing, we would ask them to put their hand on the part of the body where the

Preaching at Huruma

problem lay and then we would pray for them. It seemed like a good idea to adopt the same strategy.

As we finished I was struck by the fact that it had been so impersonal, especially if people had come a long way. For that reason, I invited a small number who felt they needed personal prayer to come forward. Hundreds came to the front. Panicking, I looked anxiously across at the interpreter. Did he translate that right? I'd said a small number. But yes, he had told them clearly enough. I could hardly believe the level of response.

At the very end of the service, someone came up to me and said, "There's someone here who knows you." I followed them to the back of the tent and there stood the air stewardess and her husband. It was at that moment that I realised that God had had this whole thing in his hands. If I had gone to Kenya on the flight

I'd wanted to catch the previous night, I would have been on a totally different plane and I would have missed her. It was part of His plan that she and I would meet each other at that time, and that she would give me that telephone number. She and her husband shared my excitement at what God was doing and strangely enough, I have never seen her again since then!

I also met an Archbishop who was doing an international conference in the largest conference centre in Nairobi. After our meeting, I ended up leading the Morning Glory prayer time at the conference centre every day.

This was my first encounter with the slum areas. The smell was overwhelming and the poverty terrible. My feet were walking one way but my whole body wanted to go in the opposite direction.

Nairobi slum

Meetings in Kawangare were small but very special as people were healed and professed salvation.

During my time in Kenya, I prayed every day that God would make it plain whether I should go back to the church in Lancing or walk away. Every night I read the following verses from Psalm 143: 8 -12. *Let the morning bring me word of your unfailing love, for I have put my trust in you. Show me the way I should go, for to you I lift up my soul.*

Right near the end of the trip as I woke one morning, as near to an audible voice as I could imagine, I heard the Lord say, "Behold, I will do a new thing; now it shall spring forth..."

I knew it was from the Bible but I didn't know whereabouts. I spent some time searching for it and yet even as I searched I was so happy. I know my Bible well and if I'd gone to it straight away, there would always be that nagging doubt that it was just part of my imagination. Eventually I found the verse in Isaiah 43 v. 19 *Behold, I will do a new thing; now it shall spring forth; shall ye not know it? I will even make a way in the wilderness, and rivers in the desert.*

Now I knew! I would not be going back to the church. I was moving on. With a heart full of worship and thanksgiving, I asked the Lord what I should tell the people at church. What was the new thing He was about to do? I felt Him say, "I'm not going to tell you. Simply say, 'God is going to do a new thing so I'm not coming back to the old thing.'"

Okay. That was fine by me and after the experience I'd just had, I felt as if I was walking on air.

Although I would never compare myself to him, I identified with the Joseph of the Bible. In fact someone at the heart of the decision-making process at that time remarked that it seemed like I was being treated like Joseph.

Joseph, misunderstood by his brothers and sold into slavery was blamed for things he had not done. Like him, I had had to handle many challenges and it was agony holding all this in. But I had decided not to complain because, I reasoned, how could God bless me if I behaved badly. I was working in the dark. Joseph would have felt the dark and dampness of the prison. However God was at work in him, despite betrayal, false promises and false accusations. It is remarkable to read how Joseph greeted his brothers later in life after their father had died. He was able to comfort them.

Genesis 50 v. 19, 20 *But Joseph said to them, "Don't be afraid. Am I in the place of God? You intended to harm me, but God intended it for good…"*

Looking back I can see how God turned that redundancy and rejection into something good for his Kingdom. Now I see and understand that God really does work all things for good. (Romans 8 v. 28) The miracle-working God who took Joseph to bless the nations was the same Lord of Heaven and earth who was about to take me all over the world. We have the same word of God to feed people with. We have the same Holy Spirit to guide us.

Since my own experience, I have been involved with many leaders and have had to suggest that they take a new direction which might be very costly for them. I have not always handled these situations as well as I would have liked, but I try to be sensitive to their feelings. Making changes in leadership is often very painful but God never gives up on us and his gifts and calling are irrevocable. Romans 11 v. 29. Praise the Lord! I thank God that so many relationships have remained intact. Elaine and I enjoyed a wonderful evening among other special guests, at a farewell to Brighton gathering, for Terry and Wendy Virgo in July 2011. It was so good to be there and to rejoice at the excellent things the Lord has done through His servants.

In 1995, the year *Living Hope Ministries* was launched, I had a chance to go to America. A Kenyan brother prayed for me to go and also funded me. While I was there, during a trip to the Greater New York area, I met Tim Storey, a gifted speaker, who was ministering at the time. He was walking around the room giving a word to various people. As I have already said, all the time I'd been going through the upheaval, I desperately struggled to be righteous and to handle it well. I knew only too well that if I gave way to bitterness and criticism I couldn't expect God's blessing on my ministry.

After a while, Tim tapped me on the back and said, "Bible teacher."

A bit later he called me out and said, "You have been working in the dark. Not many people have understood what you have handled. But God has. He has seen what you've been going through and now he sees you as his servant and He is very pleased with you. You're a Paul and God is going to be raising up Timothys through you. God's going to lift you up and your ministry is going to take-off and take-off and take-off."

Later the same year I went back to the States, this time to Chicago where I joined Kunle Omilana, a man I had met in Kenya the previous year. I thought back to Tim's prophecy and saw it as hugely significant. In the pages of this book you will meet the Timothys who have emerged from the work of *Living Hope Ministries*. And has my ministry taken off? Every time I step into yet another aeroplane and take-off for yet another new destination, I like to think so.

CHAPTER 5

Taking Shape

There were two things happening in the Christian world at this time. One was called The Toronto Blessing. This was a term coined by British churches to describe the revival and the accompanying phenomena that began in January 1994 at Toronto Airport Vineyard Christian Fellowship, now known as Toronto Airport Christian Fellowship (TACF) in Canada. Inspired by a similar revival in Argentina, John and Carol Arnott led their congregation into a freedom which brought a passion for Jesus, ecstatic worship, falling in the Spirit, laughter, shaking, and crying.

After that first trip to America, I still struggled to cope with the way people were treating me in the fellowship at home when the wider church was gong through such a time of great blessing.

When I got to Kenya, I found that the same things were happening there as in Toronto but there were two key differences. When the Toronto Blessing came to England, Christians got very excited when something amazing happened after the church service and sometimes, in order to enjoy those times, some stopped preaching the Word of God.

In Africa it was quite different. The Christians didn't say, 'Well our ministry time is over now so we'll all go home.' No matter how long they felt the need to worship the Lord, they faithfully preached the Gospel every time they met together. Their services were very, very long. And another thing, the Africans weren't so impressed by what people were doing, i.e. shaking, laughing and rolling around and such things, but when someone got up from being slain in the Spirit, they wanted to know, "What has God done in you?"

As a result, in those early days, people constantly testified to being healed of long-term illnesses. You would hear things like, "I had a growth in my tummy. I could feel it, but now it's gone!" I was reminded of the healings in the Scripture; the woman who had been bleeding for twelve years (Luke 8 v. 43-48), the man who had been lame from birth. (Acts 14 v. 7-10), and the man blind from birth (John 9 v. 1-7).

There had been a move of God in Kenya before and people were talking about Kenyan Christians and the way in which they had experienced a touch of revival. It was as if God was preparing them for the terrible unrest and tribal conflict they were to experience in the troublesome days still to come. It seems to be a fact of history that where God's people have experienced wonderful revivals, places like Rwanda and Congo, it doesn't prevent terrible things happening but it helps Christians to go through them and emerge on the other side, victorious.

In 1994/5 there was talk of Kenya being a Lighthouse to the nations but as I met and was introduced to the pastors, although they were evangelists, bringing lots of people to Christ and seeing amazing healings and masses being delivered of evil spirits and oppression, I was concerned that these men were not being taught. I was delighted to be invited to bring some of these pastors together and give them some instruction. It was that meeting that inspired the beginnings of the pastors' seminars.

Other faith groups had been in the habit of inviting African leaders to lavish breakfasts in hotels and then teaching them. I was unable to do such spectacular things but such was the hunger for the Word of God that, no matter how humble the venue, the pastors still came. After a while I felt that we had to do something more. We began by giving them bread and a Coke or a Fanta. Although it was nothing compared to what others were offering, it did emphasise that we cared about them and appreciated the fact that they had come for the Word and not what they could get.

When I got back in November 1994, it was time to put some sort of framework around what I was doing. Elaine and I prayed about the work and God gave us the name *Living Hope Ministries*. The next item on the agenda was to get *Living Hope Ministries* registered as a charity. The help Peter and Brenda Gilliver, Graham Townson and Charley Jardine gave me was invaluable.

We didn't start the procedure with a view to getting gift-aid, although that in itself has become a very important part of the ministry. No charity is registered on the nod. There has to be a great deal of investigation. You have to think through your aims and your purposes and to establish that no other charity is doing the same work. Your uniqueness has to be proven.

Peter Gilliver was a retired lecturer from Sussex University and Charley Jardine, an accountant. Between us we outlined a document, using the one we had submitted to the Charities Commission when I had been at Grace Church, as a skeleton framework for *Living Hope Ministries*. The Charities Commission gave us registration status on 21st April 1995. We called ourselves Hope in Christ serving *Living Hope Ministries*.

Initially I went for people who were really supporting me in terms of the ministry. I only approached those who could see that I had a call on my life and wanted to see the fulfilment of that call.

There is a time to pray long and hard about things but sometimes I simply know whether something is right or not. So in the early days it was a question of us gathering a group of friends together and asking them to help us put our ministry on a proper footing.

The Board of Trustees (currently Peter Lewis, Malcolm Jackson, Mike Radley, David Fordham (Chairman) and Derek Ost) look after the finances of *Living Hope Ministries*. Other people have served faithfully in this role, for which we are grateful but one brother Ray Butler and I have prayed together every week since 1995. His personal friendship and wisdom are a constant source of encouragement. Annual LHM BBQ's in his garden are greatly blessed and well supported occasions. In addition, *Living Hope Ministries* has another body of men called a Council of Reference. This is currently made up of Andrew Edwards, Andy Fadoju, Graham Jefferson, John Woods, Peter Light, and Ray Orr. (Sam Larbie,and K. Owolabi are honary members) They are more like a sounding board for the future direction and development of the ministry. They are quality friends of the sort of calibre who would not be afraid to tell me if they felt I had got anything wrong.

Thankfully, there has never been an occasion when the Council of Reference has had to admonish me, but some plans have been modified. I usually bring a seed thought, and what emerges is not always the same shape as the original idea. They constantly keep me on track and within the core vision of the work.

Once the funds that came into the work began to grow, The Board of Trustees realised they couldn't just rubberstamp everything. Every penny had to be accounted for and agreed on. Paul Newett came on board as administrator. He is a very good friend and great to bounce ideas off. Paul has brought shape and professionalism to the ministry for which we praise the Lord. Later I asked Charlene to be my personal assistant, because she was my daughter-in-law, it was important that the board of Trustees was happy with her coming and could see a genuine need in the office. Her commitment and contribution is again immensely valuable. When in 2009, Chris Lane gave up his secular work to become more fully involved with *Living Hope Ministries*, the board of Trustees, quite rightly, asked some very pertinent questions. Chris has proved to be one of those Timothy's prophesied about in 1995. He shares my heart and vision and has won the hearts of the people we work with in Living Hope.

At the beginning, I had a list of twenty-five churches that had expressed an interest in the new ministry. Any gifts they gave me went directly to fund my trips and in the early days I must have done about ten trips on my own. This was all well and good but I still didn't have a salary. The first thing I did every time I got back home was to fetch Elaine and drive straight around to the dole office. Because I had been outside the E.E.C , I had automatically lost all my benefits and I had to sign on again. I didn't like the situation, but there was no other choice. I remember crying out in frustration to the Lord many times, "Lord, I've got plenty of work but no money."

The people in the unemployment benefit office were very understanding. They never once questioned what I was doing or voiced any suspicion that I might be up to no good. The only thing that puzzled them was how a church could make me redundant. Everyone thought a Pastor's post was a job for life!

We had a mortgage, and at that time the state would pay the interest but not the capital, which at least helped to keep a roof over our heads.

Having said that, God kept providing in wonderful ways. Christmas of 1994 stands out in my memory because we were able to bless the boys more than the Christmases when I was working! I felt I was reliving 1 Kings 17 v. 10-16.[1] I can't remember anyone giving us a sizable gift, but for us, the oil jar never failed.

When I was a boy, my father was always worried about money. He hated debt and I grew up in that atmosphere. When my ability to provide was taken away, the only thing I could do was trust in the Lord. With five sons to look after, any parent will know the stresses that can bring. There's always a constant need to buy football boots, or find the money for the school trip, or school uniform. I had to put my faith and trust in God time and again because we were in that situation for four years. By the time it came to an end, we were on another benefit called Family Credit. We kept telling people that this was a faith ministry and it really troubled me that we were having to rely on the state to help keep the family. As the work grew, we decided to come off state benefits altogether and from that moment we have never looked back. Our 'wage' fluctuated. God is the only 'employer' who will pay you what you need... more when you need it and less when you don't.

Somehow He always seemed to get the timing right. Whenever we had a large bill, the money was there. If we had few needs, the giving tailed off. I often wonder how we coped, especially Elaine with the boys, but we always did.

The first time I went abroad Elaine and I knew it was right for me to go but it wasn't easy for her. Until *Living Hope Ministries* was able to support us fully, money was an issue. Each trip could cost upwards of £1,000. We both found it hard having to sign on and at one time we had a call to say that we would no longer get help to pay the interest on the mortgage.

Living by faith is not always easy, and when I'm abroad and practical things go wrong, like the time the washing machine flooded or the outside drains got blocked. It was at those times when we appreciated our wonderful neighbours and friends. Elaine and I kept in constant touch but she didn't always tell me about problems at home, especially if she thought it would worry me. Our children are just like everybody else's children and they could be difficult when I was away. Elaine is of a slight build and if the boys fought each other, she couldn't physically separate them. She recalls many a time when she had to ask the big burly Holy Spirit to help her. Life is never dull! It always took a while for the family to adjust to my being away and it took time for all of us to re-adjust to my being back.

[1] 1 Kings 17 v. 10-16 The widow of Zarephath had barely enough to feed herself and her son one last meal but Elijah the prophet asked her to bake something for him. Because she did and did it willingly, God blessed her jar of flour and her jug of oil. As a result, she and her son always had food in the house during the time of severe famine.

CHAPTER 6

Lasting Friendships

In 1996, I was in Uganda. My usual interpreter was unavailable so I was working with Pastor Dennis. He's not always the easiest person to get along with especially when he had been used to interpreting for much bigger names. As we talked by the side of the road, a man called Peter Kasozi walked by. Peter

Peter Kasozi

happened to see Dennis and he stopped to say hello and was introduced to me. Dennis invited Peter to the first conference and he kept coming along. We warmed to each other straight away.

When he was a young boy, Peter's mother died and a stepmother had brought him up. The relationship was not good and eventually she tried to poison him. In addition to that, he lived in very troubled times. In January 1971, Idi Amin Dada had deposed President Milton Obote and taken power in a military coup. Amin's rule was characterised by hundreds of human rights' abuses, political repression, murders and the compulsory expulsion of the Asian community from the country. It's not known exactly how many people lost their lives during his reign of terror but estimates range from 100,000 to 500,000.

There was an occasion when Peter himself was caught up in the terror. At one time, when the army were rounding up people for execution, Peter happened to be standing near one of the trucks. Someone grabbed his arm and he was about to be taken when another man said, "He's too young." His captor let go of his arm and Peter was able to run away.

There was another occasion when Peter was hiding in the roof space of a house when the soldiers came. He heard soldiers go into the house next door and then they fired many shots into the roof. The soldiers came into the house where he was hiding, looked around but thank God, they didn't fire into the roof.

Peter has known what it's like to beg on the street for his very survival. Life for him as a child was never easy, but it gave him a real heart for children. Although I personally think his main ministry is an apostolic one, church planting and the like, Peter devotes himself to the children in his care. He is now a director of a large school with 1,000 children at Kitetikka, and as an established church leader, he also had a burden for pastors to be trained. As a result, there was a real sense of connection between us both.

Peter once told me that the thing he liked about me, is that I try to get to know people personally. I have often been able to remember names and judging by the reaction of other people, I think it must be a gift because I seldom struggle to place a face or a name. I always supposed that my days as a teacher must have trained my mind to recall names and faces, but perhaps God has gifted me to go over and above the natural. I can even remember African names. I may not always spell them correctly, but I can remember them!

Many Westerners set off to foreign climes with great zeal but they don't have the stamina for long haul. Within a few years of my coming to Uganda, Peter realised that I really was going to keep on being involved in the country even though I was going to other places. He understood the sacrifice and he saw my obedience to God and he has told me he valued that. I suppose it's because I make up my mind to try and understand the community ethos wherever I happen to be. I think it's important not to arrive with pre-set ideas and try to do things my way. I need to find out about the people and the culture and more importantly, what they have been going through. I realised early on that I need to preach in a way which is relevant to them and their situation and which is of practical help for them. Everybody needs encouragement, but the kind of encouragement that helps a middle class English Christian worrying about mortgage rates, and which school to send his children, will not be of any use to an African living in a slum with no regular job.

We must be doing something right because after fifteen years or more going to Africa, the people have grown to love and respect the *Living Hope Ministries* conferences. These days they get to hear about the meetings by mobile phone but in the beginning the host churches contacted people by letter, radio announcement, postcards or word of mouth.

By working together, Peter and I have both fulfilled our own personal vision. Through the ministry of *Living Hope*, Peter has been encouraged in his zeal for church planting, and our shared vision is the building up of the pastors. During times of revival, when people turn to the Lord, the leadership has to be in place. In the West, if someone feels called to be a leader, he or she will go to a Bible college for a period of time and then be offered a church or a junior role in a larger church. The same thing happens in Africa with the more established churches because they have been there long enough to have set up the same kind of system. But with the more indigenous people, a person may go to a village to preach, and thirty or forty people may come to the Lord. Didn't Jesus say, *"I tell you, open your eyes and look at the fields! They are ripe for harvest."* John 4 v. 35 That person, the one who first took the Good News, of necessity becomes the leader of those he has brought to Christ. Other churches may be many miles away and the people so poor their only means of travel is on foot, so even if he wanted to filter them into the more established churches, it becomes impossible. They need Church in their own village.

Some of these itinerate preachers have some education, little education or are illiterate. They certainly have no materials, nor the funds to buy them. If people like *Living Hope Ministries* are not there to support the evangelist and his group, they can easily fall prey to cults or cultish practices. The evangelist himself may not even be based in a church. He may have simply heard the call of God and gone out straight away with the Good News. The one good thing about the people is that, because they are so keen, they will accept help. Most evangelists live by faith, although some have a job and work for God in their spare time. Although Peter and his associates do not dictate what any evangelist should do, they do encourage them to work at something else to support themselves. 1 Tim 5 v. 8 *If anyone does not provide for his relatives, and especially for his immediate family, he has denied the faith and is worse than an unbeliever.*

Uganda is a country on the up. It has a steady expansion of road building, and up-to-date communications and other vital infrastructures. This has brought a corresponding increase in international tourist arrivals and upmarket facilities. Many come to see the endangered mountain gorilla, the largest of all living primates, but perhaps the most peaceable. Uganda is a country with thirty-plus different indigenous languages belonging to five distinct linguistic groups, and an equally diverse cultural mosaic of music, art and handicrafts.

Since I have been going to Uganda, I have seen that change taking place. In the beginning there was an atmosphere of fear and oppression left over from the Amin and Obote years. Many pastors had been killed under those regimes.

Relative peace came with the new leadership under Yoweri Museveni, but as time went on, extreme cults have mushroomed; the most infamous being that of the World Message Last Warning Church. Around 1,000 followers sold all their belongings and set up camp near Luwero. The Ugandan police arrested several members of the cult and charged them with rape and kidnapping, but not before they had given everything they owned to cult leader Wilson Bushara.

If that was bad, there was worse to come. In March 2000, members of the Movement for the Restoration of the Ten

Commandments Church gathered in Kangngu. Their pastor Joseph Kibwetere who had founded the church in the late 1980s persuaded his people that they would receive a blessing if they were anointed with oil. With no oil available, the leaders used petrol instead. Somehow, no one quite knows why, a fire started. To their horror, the people, 530 in all, found that the doors were locked and the windows had been nailed shut. The tragedy seems to have been deliberate because later on Ugandan police found the bodies of another 380 cult members, hidden under houses or thrown down wells or the toilet pits.

It came as no surprise then, when at one meeting I had a feeling that there were people present who had actually taken life. I was surprised however, when at the altar call as many as 50-60 people came up. For a few minutes I wondered if there had been a breakdown in translation but the look on Peter's face told me the people had perfectly understood what I had said. I had never expected the numbers to be so high. We prayed with those people as they repented of their wrongdoing and sought to put things right. Some needed deliverance from the memories of nightmare situations.

Having such a close friendship with Peter means that when I hear something on the news, I feel personally involved with the country. For instance, when I heard that a building had collapsed just outside Kampala killing at least ten people and trapping many more, I rang him to express my sorrow. My condolences were made even more poignant when I realised that he knew some of the Christian leaders gathered for prayer, who had lost their lives. Sadly this kind of thing happens all too frequently. Construction companies cut corners by using substandard materials or insufficient cement. The situation was made even more real to us when one of the Pastors came to our seminars on crutches.

I once asked Stephen Kiguru from Kenya to tell me when I sounded 'English.' I wanted to share the gospel but I didn't want to teach African Christians to be English Christians. That's not to say that I would ever want to water down the gospel in any way, but I always need to be sensitive to the African culture and to see things from their point of view.

The question is often asked, how do the Africans deal with people who have gone through a trauma? Well, in the same way as the Western church uses counselling and prayer, so does the African. They talk and pray with people in just the same way but the problems may not be the same as the Westerner might encounter. In Africa they deal with witchcraft and a lot of what we would call, actual bodily harm. The Spirit of God helps them to discern and He teaches them how to help each other.

The African believer is often better able to identify if someone has been involved in witchcraft. During a visit to the UK, I invited Peter to come with me to an Alpha course. Although he didn't expose the person to shame, he immediately identified someone who had been involved in some way with the occult. That knowledge was a powerful weapon when dealing with any issues the Alpha course may have thrown up in that person's life. Peter's experience is much sharper when it comes to enemy activity and the power of God. He is better able to discern these things.

"The one good thing that the Westerner has done," Peter says, "is to give themselves to study. The African lights one candle and goes everywhere with it, but people from the UK have had the study of many generations embedded in their culture. They are grounded in the Word."

This is exactly how I feel. There are men and women who have been sitting on the pew for twenty, thirty, or forty years. They have heard the gospel but they have never taken the opportunity to go out and share it. Perhaps they've never had the opportunity. Perhaps they think it's all too late now. Perhaps they don't believe they could do it. Well, I have the good news and the bad news. Maybe it's all of those things, but the good news is that the Holy Spirit will give you the opportunities, it's never too late, and you can do all things through Christ.

"The only caution I would voice," Peter goes on to say, "is that if one studies for too long a time, one might feel 'I've reached it'. The African comes to the Bible as if he has heard it for the first time. He reads one thing and has to rush out and tell someone, he's so excited."

It's easy to feel discouraged that so much of our heritage has been lost in this day and age, but I know Peter has been blessed when he has come to this country and seen young people on fire for God. There was an occasion when he and I were in a Bible bookshop together. We met a young man and his wife who truly loved God and I know Peter enjoyed the simple pleasure of watching their enthusiasm.

Another thing, which has helped me become respected among the African brothers, is the places where I'm willing to stay. They are not typical of the places English people choose. It took a while before the Africans I worked with came to realise that not every white man is rich. The transport I was willing to use was also different. Not many tourists would be keen to use bicycle taxi. Take a bicycle and place a thin padded seat behind the saddle. That's a bicycle taxi. The passenger sits sideways and the rider peddles like mad. You may make slow progress but you get there in the end. I've been in cars where the windscreen is shattered and sometimes I've even wondered if the car doors are going to stay on! Our brothers come to realise that I'm willing to travel like this, not because I'm mean, but because my means are limited. And it's been quite an education for them to discover that white people are willing to give something more to a situation than just money.

God used Peter to open the media door for *Living Hope Ministries* in Uganda. It was Peter who introduced me to someone from Lighthouse TV. By that introduction, people have been made aware of Peter's school and some have come forward to sponsor a child. The television introductions led *Living Hope Ministries* to Family TV Kenya, Top Radio and Impact Radio giving us access to a much larger audience.

Peter and Rose Kasozi

Because we have become a family, I have shared the needs of some of the brothers with other churches. When Peter was going through a particularly hard time, I asked the brothers in Romania to pray for him. I didn't give any details, that would have been unnecessary and inappropriate, but as we prayed, one man has a vision. He said he saw Peter weeping, and as the tears hit the ground, the plants began to grow. These brothers knew nothing about Peter's trials but the Holy Spirit had spoken through them. What they shared gave encouragement to Peter, bonded us together as brothers and both 'words' proved to be prophetic. God did allow a great deal of Peter's support to ebb away, but since then he has built Peter and his wife up again. The school flourishes, and his work continues.

Our friendship has been tested but we have worked it through and because of that, we feel we are true friends. And isn't this the test of true friendship? That you stick with people even though you may have some differences of opinion.

Sadly, sometimes we come to a real parting of the ways. That happened to Dennis, the man who introduced me to Peter. Dennis was eager to lend a hand when we needed an interpreter but right from the start, there was a misunderstanding. Dennis thought that it meant he was my co-ordinator but as far as I was concerned, it never was that way. I had only asked him to stand in while my usual interpreter wasn't around.

Dennis is a good man. Although he could see that people came and heard the word of God, because of the way I work, there was no money in it and that left him on the horns of a dilemma. If he stayed, he would remain penniless but if he ditched me publicly, there may have been a backlash because everyone was so obviously enjoying the message.

As with any organisation, dealing with people and seeking to fund various projects, we often encounter problems. It's sometimes hard to keep your spirit sweet in the face of false accusation, innuendo and suspicion.

In the search for funding, an African pastor came into contact with a church in the UK. One lady became a sort of mother figure to him. She raised funds for the school but after a while questions were raised. The school had been built on the pastor's ancestral land and he understandably struggled with the idea that he should hand everything over to people in a faraway country. After all, his ancestral lands had been entrusted to him for future generations of his own family.

The African way of doing things is very different from the way we do things in the West. There were unreasonable demands. On one occasion when he was in the UK with a choir, the African pastor was asked to empty his pockets so that the church could filter everything and anything he might have been given. Thus the level of trust and the pastor's dignity were greatly undermined.

Our African friends know the westerner's need for receipts but in Uganda if you ask for a receipt, the person will say, "How much do you want me to make it out for?" In other words, it doesn't mean anything. The mindset and the culture are totally different. To us in the West, a receipt is a measure of integrity, but to the African there are other ways of showing your integrity. At the end of the day you either trust someone or you don't.

I remember once having a conversation with an African pastor who had a position of high office in local government. During his time in office, he had a very strange visit from some local people. They had no idea that the man was a born again Christian, and in the course of conversation they openly confessed that they were witches. They also had a hidden agenda, and explained that they would go to any lengths to carry it out. "We're actively praying that people in the West who support Christians will stop doing it," they said. "If they do, we will be able to stamp out Christianity more easily."

When I hear of such corrosive things, I am convinced that there may be an element of witchcraft involved. Whatever the reason, the sad thing is the good work that particular church was doing in Uganda was nearly destroyed.

A little later, when our friend, Trevor Bond came out to Uganda, he gave that particular pastor a prophetic word. Trevor had no idea about the situation but he told him, "A fire has come and taken everything away, but God is going to bless you and restore everything back."

We must avoid at all costs any semblance of Christian colonialism. We are called to serve, bless and support. Yes, accountability is important, but it should come out of relationship and mutual respect, not imposition.

CHAPTER 7

Passing Ships

Some people join *Living Hope Ministries* and move on to another venture. I am happy about that. It increases ministry and as long as we behave righteously it means that the people of God are having their needs met in all sorts of ways. It takes the pressure off to be all things to all people. Some folk continue to relate closely; others go their own way. God has given me a specific calling and I can follow that to the letter, trusting Him to call others into other needy situations. One such a man who still relates closely, is Anton Green. Anton came out to Kenya with me for the first time in 1997. Arriving in Nairobi very early in the morning, having flown all night, we went straight to a conference in Buru Buru hosted by Joseph Omollo. Joseph was a dear man and Anton taught him the rudiments of managing money. As I have already intimated, so many Africans think all people from the west are very rich. I suppose by their standards we are, but they have no concept of how expensive things are in Britain. *Living Hope Ministries* has limited resources and we had to use them as carefully as we could.

The conference was held at the home church of Stephen Kiguru and later in the day we went to Joseph's church. This was Anton's first encounter with the other Africa, the Africa of the slums and the plight of ordinary people in their daily struggle for survival.

At that time Joseph had given up a good job with the Kenyan Electricity Company to serve the Lord more fully. He was living in a house with just two tiny rooms, with his wife and two children.

I went with Anton to Uganda, a beautiful lush green country with a sky full of soaring birds, although I have to confess that when he pointed out that the sky was full of storks, falcons, and vultures hovering on the thermals, I hadn't really noticed. My mind was totally focussed on the conference and so he was taken aback when I said, "Is it, Anton?"

We arrived in Entebbe in blazing sunshine but by the time we got out of the airport buildings the light had gone. It is a feature of Africa that there is no twilight. One minute it is light and the next it's pitch black. As there was nobody there to meet us, I could sense that he was worried so I suggested a time of prayer.

"Dear Lord, we've arrived. We would like someone to come and connect with us, Amen."

We were to meet up with Pastor Dennis, but within twenty minutes Peter Kasozi came with his wife to pick us up in a car and we set off for Kampala. We hadn't been going along very far before we hit something in the road, severely damaging the tyre. Peter opened the boot for a spare but it was empty. He didn't seem to be too concerned but none of us could imagine where we could possibly get help.

After a few minutes we heard a 'put-put-put' sound and out of the darkness came a man on a tiny moped. Without further ado, Peter hailed this person, leapt on the pillion seat with the wheel, and disappeared into the night, leaving Anton and myself with his wife Rose.

I could see that Anton was concerned by sounds in the night. Me too! There was movement in the darkness and we saw the occasional light. Given the past history of the country, I said jokingly, "If our two wives knew where we were, I don't think they'd be too happy about it."

"I don't think they would," Anton agreed

We made polite conversation with Rose until Peter reappeared with the repaired wheel. It wasn't until we were on our way, that we realised that after nightfall the roadside becomes a continuous market. People were everywhere, buying and selling.

We finally arrived at Pastor Dennis' house and once we got to bed, within a minute or two of my head hitting the pillow, I fell fast asleep. The next morning, refreshed by my sleep, I discovered that Anton had been awake half the night, disturbed by drums from a traditional wedding in the compound next door. I hadn't heard a thing!

We went to Kibanda where Dennis had built a church, but it was unfinished. It had walls and a roof but nothing more. However, it was a good sized floor area and we had a full five day conference there. As I have mentioned before, Dennis wasn't the easiest of men to deal with but Anton rose to the challenge and I could see that he was already working out a better way of doing things. As a result, *Living Hope Ministries* made provision for those who wanted to stay overnight, and to feed the delegates. We also organised benches to sit on and for a public address system to be laid on at the church.

By 1999, under Anton's administration, the treasurer back home was very happy with the planning and what we had done.

One of the most significant people we met was Atwina Allen Knight. After Idi Amin was deposed in Uganda, Milton Obote ruled until 1985, when an army brigade, commanded by Lt. Gen. Bazilio Olara-Okello, took Kampala and proclaimed a military government. Uganda lurched back from a mad dictatorship to a repressive regime held in check only by anarchy. Yoweri Museveni, one time Uganda's minister of defence during the interim government after the fall of Amin, went into the bush with twenty other patriots and formed a guerrilla group, subsequently known as the National Resistance Army. Basing itself on organizational discipline, his army didn't pillage and rape and they introduced a much more stable government.

In her younger days Atwina Allen Knight had been caught up in that upheaval. As a teenager she had been a lieutenant and had driven into Kampala in a truck but after a life-changing experience, now she was helping *Living Hope Ministries*.

Atwina had a real gift for administration. The team would make a decision about how many Bibles they needed in English and Ugandan and then Atwina would drive Anton into Kampala,

which is quite a big city, and find the best price from the various
Christian book shops.

Peter Kasozi was also very generous and put his vehicle at our
disposal. He would work tirelessly to prepare everything for us
before we came. We went into the cattle region of the north west of
Uganda, an area which at the time was not as politically stable as
other parts. At Lake Albert, we discovered that only two years
before there had been a raid in the village, and forty people had
been killed. One pastor had lost twelve cattle which was a huge
blow to him.

During the conference we had people speaking five different
languages and so we had to have five different interpreters. At
times there was a sense of spiritual warfare but we weren't really
frightened. At a place called Kyebando we came across a church
where the members felt they were under attack. Someone had been
found murdered on the site and the people were quite concerned,
but we lifted the situation to the Lord and we believe that God
answered prayer.

It's a testimony to God's protection and power that even in
Kibera, one of the most prominent slums of the area around
Nairobi, where it wouldn't be wise to walk around on our own, we
were more than happy to walk with some trusted brothers. I firmly
believe that anyone coming to Africa should take the time to see
the conditions people live in.

In Katrari there is an area where the people have an illegal
still. The beverage they brew has been known to make a man go
blind, but such is the emotional pain of the people, they drink it to
blot out their misery. Visitors are not welcome. In fact when David
Weaver went there in 2008 he carried a camera and when he tried
to film them, the people threw stones at him.

Anton has two sons and a daughter, and his son was in
Zambia at exactly the same time as Anton was in Kenya and
Uganda, such is the passion his family has for the people of Africa.
Although he has done several trips with *Living Hope Ministries*, God

has moved Anton on to another project. Since his first visit and his encounter with true poverty, he has developed a relationship with a man called John Obayo. John, a member of the Luo tribe was a single man, tall about 30 years old, rather thoughtful and dignified. He ran the conferences for me in the slums and is still part of *Living Hope Ministries* Kenya. Together they have set up a small business support project which finances people in John's church, a tiny shack, dark, mud walled with thirty-five people crammed inside. It costs them £10 a month to rent and it was also used as a schoolroom. Only a few of the congregation had jobs, among them a night watchmen and someone who broke up stones at a quarry. In a place like that, nobody can give a tithe to support the ministry and so on paper the situation looked hopeless. Yet the people really believed God and loved Him.

John's home was equally humble. He was a single man but he was looking after four orphan children, none of whom were his own. Their parents had been killed in a car crash, something which is common-place in Kenya, where the traffic is totally unregulated.

"I can never forget," Anton says with a pained expression, "walking into Kibera and following this channel of evil smelling liquid which ran right beside these grotty homes of wattle and dawb with tin roofs. How could I possibly walk away and do nothing?"

My calling was to support pastors in those kinds of situations but the Lord was showing Anton something else. For his 50th birthday Anton had a party, and instead of having presents, he asked his friends to give money to help this church in Kwantara. He recieved £1200!

Through the generosity of his church and his friends back home, Anton had already helped John Obayo to set up a sewing cooperative with five sewing machines and an overlocker. John calls it The Salvation Gospel Church Christian Sewing and Tailoring School and it operates out of a shack in Kibera. Anton gave the birthday money to John, trusting him to use some of it for his own needs and some of it for the church.

John contacted him a while later to say that he was getting married. When Anton realised he had used some of the money for a dowry, he was at first a bit affronted. *Living Hope Ministries* has helped many of us back home come to understand that 'our' way is not always the best way. If we want to trust our brothers to do what is best for themselves, then we have to have a hands-off approach. Ah, you say, what if they abused that trust? Then so be it. We have given money in good faith and we are all on a learning curve, the African too. On further reflection, Anton realised that in fact, John was doing a wonderful thing. Up until then John had been unable to marry Grace, his childhood sweetheart and now those four orphans had a mother. Now John and Grace have a little boy of their own. The rest of the money was used to pay the rent for the church building and buy a PA system. John was now supported in full-time ministry and the small business support group was started. The participants are trained before they are given a part-grant, part-loan to get them started. The grant is generous and once the people have paid back their loan and have enough stock, they move into stage two when they get a further loan and grant to help them reach a stage of self-sufficiency. These businesses are, by our standards, forms of street hawking, like selling second-hand shoes, butchering, rearing chickens or selling bulk cereals or fish. For these people they are the difference between life and death.

Anton has mostly been in Kenya and Uganda both in the cities and further up country. Like most of the *Living Hope Ministries* preachers and teachers, he has never been to a game reserve or to the tourist locations.

Another man who has moved on to other things is John Ray. John came with me on several trips in the 1990s and he made a video about *Living Hope Ministries* called *A Heart for Africa*. It was very useful to use as a tool when I went around the churches. On one occasion, this time with Bernard Lord and Anton Green, we made a very brief visit to Kitetikka and John made a video of the school. After a while John turned his attention to another project.

He now heads up Hope for Lugazi which has been instrumental in buying land and building a school as well as finding funding for forty-five children. The foundation stone of the school, a magnificent building and built to western standards, was laid by Graham Jefferson, another of the *Living Hope Ministries* Council of Reference.

Africa gets you that way...

CHAPTER 8

Into Radio and Television

Having seen the tremendous effect a radio programme can have, I rang David McQuarrie in 1998, and asked him if he would consider doing some TV programmes for Africa. Although he confessed that he had never done anything like it before, I was confident of his reputation. Coming from a career in insurance, David, who had only become a Christian in 1993, had been filming other people's family celebrations for ten years.

David, and his then next-door neighbour, Carole along with another cameraman, Adrian, had done several weddings at Arun Christian Fellowship. It was through someone at Arun that David had become a Christian and after he was made redundant when the Brighton office of his insurance company closed, someone had suggested, "Why don't you turn your hobby into a business."

When he began filming for *Living Hope Ministries*, David was only using VHS tapes and the recording was rather primitive because he couldn't edit them, and they didn't copy very well. This meant that my talks had to be done 'live'. David and Carole would arrive with a pile of tapes, each with a prepared intro, which they had paused. As soon as they gave me the thumbs up, they would begin to record and I would start speaking. If I made a mistake it was too bad. We couldn't do much about it, apart from starting all over again.

When they first started working together, Carole was plunged in the deep end. She hadn't done any camera work before but they worked well together, using sign language between them to get by.

"Once you make a mistake," Carole would laugh as she glanced over her shoulder at David, "you'll never make the same mistake again!"

Carole is now a qualified Master Member in her own right with the Institute of Videography. For those in the know, this is the best industry recommendation that you can have. Both David and Carole are both part of the Association of Professional Video makers so I was doubly blessed to have them aboard. They began by upgrading their own equipment. There were various changes but they ended up with four cameras. As their wedding work tailed off, they did more work for *Living Hope Ministries*, which is actually very generous of them, because even though I pay the 'going rate', they don't make a lot of money. Carole maintained her full-time job teaching people from day nurseries and working in child-care, in order to pay the bills. She had a great sense of humour and she loved teasing her husband. "David? He's a kept man," she would say gleefully.

With no experience of public broadcasting, I instinctively knew when to stop or wrap up a message. When I'd finished the talk, I sometimes asked David, "Is that OK?" but he'd be so absorbed in getting the right shot, he hadn't really taken in what I'd said. I understand that. Like me, David has developed a sort of tunnel vision and could blot everything else out so that he was able to concentrate on the job in hand.

It was obvious that this enthusiastic couple got a terrific buzz out of their work and loved to talk about the work they'd done. As the years went on, they swapped roles. David did the main camera and Carole did all the mixing.

Since we began working together, Carole developed a second sense and could often predict what I was about to do. Still, there were some things even she couldn't predict. Like the time David sneezed in the middle of a filming session and we had to stop and start again.

"Shall we play the film back," said Carole, "so that you can pick it up again?"

"No, carry on," I said.

"But you may have lost your train of thought," she insisted.

"I'll be fine," I smiled.

When we had finished, they were amazed that to see that the change over was seamless. Whenever I stopped, I could carry on exactly from where I left off. Of course, timing is of the essence and we got it right most of the time because they were so professional at what they did. They had an instinct and I trusted in them. Occasionally we were hampered by my dry cough, but that only happened if we'd been doing several talks at the same time.

Sometimes they wanted to try anything new. That was fine by me. If it didn't work out, I was quite willing to redo it. There was a time when we were doing some talks in my office (a rather grand name for my garage). I was sitting beside a light at my desk. We had been plagued by a buzzing sound on the recordings but we had completed three programmes before we discovered that it was the dimmer switch on the light causing the problem.

The technical advances have made a great difference to copying the programmes. With the advent of DVDs it takes much less time and it costs a lot less. David and Carole fill in the media sheets and we've got 'endings' which may be a piece of music or a short conclusion from someone else (one of the team) to round off the broadcast.

It grieves me to think of the way some Christians have treated David and Carole. They've worked for many other Christian organisations and they never charged very much but sadly not everyone has honoured them with their wage. People want the goods but are reluctant to pay. "You'll get blessed in heaven," is an oft bandied quote, but that doesn't pay their mortgage. I felt very strongly that *Living Hope Ministries* should pay David and Carole as soon as the work was done and so, whenever we had a filming session, I always came prepared with the cheque book.

If you watch Christian TV invariably it's an interview or a church service. The person speaking doesn't look at the camera. He or she looks at someone off camera. I prefer to look straight down the lens as if I'm talking to that person and I give basic Bible teaching. I'm not in the game of promoting myself, or my products. I only want to get the gospel message into people's homes and to change their lives. The Philippians love this. They would have our programmes on TV all day.

The first time Carole went abroad with *Living Hope Ministries* the team went to Kenya, Uganda and Rwanda where Carole filmed just about everything she could. At the same time as filming for me, Carole was also making a film for the World Health Organisation.

The last day we were there, I was feeling very unwell and because my confidence is always in the protecting power of God, I had taken few medicines. On the other hand, Carole was a walking chemist shop, and on that occasion, I received my protection from her forethought and generosity.

Carole came with me as part of the team in 2003 as well. This second time she made a TV programme about the trip. It was fraught with problems. One church had a corrugated iron roof and during the service we had a rain storm. The noise was unbelievable and of course it made it very difficult to get good sound quality.

Sadly, much as she wanted to, it was difficult for Carole to film because it was too dangerous. There was one occasion when the most amazing thing happened. As we drove from Uganda to Rwanda we had to queue up for passport inspection. A man walked over to our car and asked us if we were Christians. We told him we were. Oh dear. What was he up to? Was he nursing a hatred towards Christians? Was he a troublemaker?

The man looked me straight in the eye. "I want to become a Christian, too," he said.

Another time on that same trip, we broke down and the whole team had to spend the night in the car.

"Anyone got a mobile?" I asked. But nobody had.

It wasn't the best place to be although no-one was really afraid. All through the night, big banana lorries thundered by buffeting the car. We had little sleep. In the distance, we could hear drumming and someone pointed out that they were probably the Batwa, people who in the past had been branded crop raiders, beggars and even cannibals. Before she came out on that mission, Carole had a strange dream. She told me she had dreamt that we had been captured by cannibals. They had two pots. I was in one pot and she was in the other! Thankfully, everyone survived that night completely unscathed but when the tow-truck finally arrived to rescue us, it had run out of petrol. For anyone who has ever been there, you will know what I mean when I say, "That's Africa for you!"

One time, coming back from having a shower in North Uganda, the team was met by some angry looking men with guns. Thankfully, our guide spoke their language and pacified the men, and they were quick to apologise. They had thought that we were game rustlers.

Even though we all took great care of ourselves, one of the team came back to England covered in flea bites. We had to be aware of so many unsafe things. For instance, bananas are the safest fruit. If you eat any other piece of fruit, it may have been washed in some very suspect water. Bottled water in some African countries is not always sterilised, so care must be taken when buying bottled water. Chips are safe to eat. If they are deep fried in hot fat

Staple diet!

that will kill all the bugs. I'm not a great lover of foreign food. My idea of a good meal is Sunday roast... but you can't get that in Africa. Everyone knows I like chips so I quite often get them!

Drinking the milk in Rwanda is risky for the Westerner only used to having pasteurised milk. Having said that, we had to be very careful not to offend people. They may have been poor but they were very generous and often whatever they offer you, would have been given sacrificially. It's a good maxim to remember, don't ask what you're eating, say grace and just eat it.

Living Hope Ministries now broadcasts in Kenya, Nigeria, India and Uganda. These programmes are seen by millions of people, and judging by the email responses, they are having a real effect on both believers and non Christians. In reality these programmes compliment my visits but they also reach many more people than I could ever do in person. Our programmes are extremely popular both in Africa and the UK because of their straightforward Bible teaching and have been shown free of charge on the satellite channel.

In June 2005 the Churches Media Council awarded one of David and Carole's television programmes, filmed for the Living Word Temple in Tottenham, a 'commendation'. This film included footage that Carole shot in Rwanda on a *Living Hope Ministries* trip when she visited the genocide sites. The programme was made, ostensibly, to highlight the need for orphanages in Africa where so many children have no living parents. Understandably, at the award ceremony, the BBC walked away with most of the awards but then their budget is somewhat different. During the award ceremony, ex-choir boy and now radio and TV presenter, Aled Jones was sitting opposite Carole.

"So," he asked, leaning towards her and smiling brightly, "how much is your budget and how many people are you?"

"Well, there's me, Dave and Mike," said Carole, "and as for my budget, if I'm lucky, I might get a sandwich on the M25!"

What a shame she wasn't filming. Aled's jaw dropped!

David has now retired but before doing so, he sold his equipment to *Living Hope Ministries* at a very generous rate. He also helped to launch a much younger team consisting of Matthew Newett, Charlene Brunton and my son Matthew into this worldwide ministry, which takes the gospel into so many countries.

CHAPTER 9

A year in the Life of Living Hope Ministries

In 1999, as the world was gearing itself to go into another century, my life was falling into a regular pattern.

In April I went to Uganda and Kenya. The Tourist Board calls Uganda Africa's friendliest country. Entebbe is a modern and efficient international airport, situated near Lake Victoria which itself boasts a golf course leading down to the lakeshore, and a century-old botanical garden complete with monkeys and tropical birds. Uganda's star attraction is undoubtedly the endangered mountain gorilla, but as I only had two weeks in the country, I had little time for visiting such places.

On this occasion, I had the pleasure of being accompanied by Anton Green and John Ray.

I'd first met Anton in 1996/7. His youngest son had reached his mid-teens and so Anton felt it was time for him to branch out
a bit and do something a little more challenging than the daily routine of work through the week and church on Sunday.

As I have already said, the first trip we made together was in1998 to Kenya and Uganda and his first responsibility was to manage the moneybag. He was initially overwhelmed by conditions in the third world but as with many of us, it isn't long before Africa with its wonderful tapestry of colourful human life and fascinating people, lays a hold on your heart and imagination.

A modest man, Anton is a social worker by profession, and responsible for the management of social workers. In Africa, people look for a person with status in the church, but Anton went to great pains to tell everybody he was just an ordinary member of his church. He had been asked to speak at his church two or three times a year but he felt he didn't really have a call to preach. The first time he went, although the Africans were keen to hear him speak, he preferred to talk to the children in the Sunday schools.

John Ray was never sure quite how he ended up going with us but I had preached in his church, New Life, Durrington and his Pastor, Rev. Graham Jefferson, was on the council of Reference. At the time, John was freelance, making videos, and so the plan was that he should video the sights and sounds of the conference and share them with a wider audience not only in the UK but also in Africa. After a conversation he had with Pastor Jason Egesa, John was keen to offer the videos for use as outreach for the people in villages in Kenya. He also spent some time exploring the whole idea of Broadcast TV. He told me he had a desire to help the African brothers keep their own cultural identity and we both agreed that we should aim for a more balanced output, which featured Ugandan nationals.

John remarked on how focussed I was. I hit the ground running and keep going which is why I can only go for ten days or so at a time, because I use up so much energy. My attitude has always been, I'm only here for a little while and I will do as much as I can in the timespan.

John had been to Africa before but this was his first time with *Living Hope Ministries*. Nonetheless when I wrote the itinerary, I included John as a speaker at the Kyebando Conference in Uganda. At first he wasn't very confident about that but gradually he realised that he only needed to be willing and if he dipped into all the teaching he had received over the years, the Holy Spirit would lead the way! The conference was held in a large building. It had walls and a roof but the floor was earth and there were no furnishings! Everything for the delegates, about 350 of them, had to be brought in. From a budget of £2000, raised in the UK, we provided food for everyone, hired and transported benches and mattresses for sleeping, a power hook-up and a generator for the PA system. We also had to freshen up the toilet facilities which meant pumping out the cesspit. Anton carried all the money for this in a pouch around his neck.

It always amazed and encouraged me that God's people gave so generously. Not only had we taken cash to pay for everything but we were also able to extend our giving to the people of Africa. On this trip, we expanded our suitcases to accommodate 256 Bibles, 40 of which we gave out in Kenya, and 216 in Uganda. We gave out 200 Bible commentaries, which were donated by a trust in Ipswich, 6 Lion Bible Handbooks and 6 Bible Dictionaries. We also gave out hundreds of Bible studies; pictures for children to colour; and many worship tapes, all of which had been donated.

We used the rest of the money gifts to enable us to pay for the installation of a telephone for the office in Kenya, buy some PA equipment for *Living Hope Ministries* Kenya and install electricity for the host church in Kampala.

Many evangelists and teachers travelling to Africa give little thought to the welfare of the people gathering to hear them. I was convinced that God wanted me to take care of his sheep, not only to feed them spiritually but also to look after their bodies. For that reason, apart from what we had already done, we fed the conference delegates for a week, some of whom had travelled 200 miles to hear God's Word.

The women of the church prepared the meals, usually out in the open on charcoal fires. The meals consisted of rice, some meat and Githeri. This is a mixture of boiled maize and beans, a popular dish among the Kikuyu community. Sometimes they ate Mukimo, a mashed version of the Githeri, made up of maize and beans mashed with potatoes or cooked bananas, or Matoke, a Ugandan speciality.

Clearly the people we were called to serve had no money for accommodation, so rather than leave them to sleep on the ground out in the open, through the local church, we provided mattresses for them as well.

The Kenyan conferences were well attended with some 140 pastors making their way to Buru Buru, and their responses and reports proved to be very encouraging.

Later on we got down to the business side of *Living Hope Ministries* and held a trustees' meeting of *Living Hope Ministries* Kenya. Afterwards, the ministry was officially registered with the Kenyan government. A fantastic step forward.

It was good to know that Pastors Joseph and Salmon would be following us to Kampala as we needed to release Bishop Stephen unexpectedly. At that time, Stephen was the overseer of the Full Gospel Churches of Kenya and his daughter, who is now married and living in Finland, was studying there.

In Pastor Moses' new church in Kampala, they had made an excellent start with 15-20 people, and there was a keen sense of God's presence. I enjoy speaking to small groups of people as much as to the crowds.

Later, Moses took me to Top Radio, a Christian radio station. The crowded building, little more than a house, was full of life and very busy. After I had been interviewed, to my great surprise and delight, I was offered a regular programme slot and I signed up for 15 minutes per month. If that wasn't exciting enough, when I got back home to the UK, I discovered that the people from the URC church, Lewes Road, Brighton, had been in touch with Elaine to ask for a project they could support. Although Elaine did not know what was happening in Uganda, she suggested the media work of *Living Hope Ministries*. As a result, the church's gift paid the first year's costs of that broadcast!

The move into the medium of television for our African brothers was also fairly amazing. Bishop Peter Kasozi had invited a friend called Jennifer, a woman who went on to become a politician, to come and hear me speak. She came to a meeting at Kwampe, a district pastored by Pastor Dennis, the man whose services as an interpreter were often used by speakers coming to Kampala.

On that 1999 trip, funds were diverted from some of the advanced money sent to set up the conference on a grandiose scheme to build new toilets in a swamp behind the church. I guess someone thought it would be a good idea but it did mean that we arrived without among other things, any power in the church.

When we arrived, Anton chalked up the budget on a blackboard and got together with David Livingstone Wuhalia, Atwina Allen Knight, Solomon Biromumaiso, Javia Binomugisha and Mark Wamuhalla to talk everything through. Everyone was fantastic. Dennis found it difficult to participate in this more open approach but he came round in the end and was pleased with the outcome.

We were well received at Lighthouse Television, and the programme seemed to make a distinctive contribution. The dust, the heat and the bustle of an African slum was a world away from the closed doors of the air-conditioned and well-organised studio. Lighthouse wasn't rich by our standards but it was in stark contrast to life outside. Their funding comes from an incredibly generous church in the USA and Joyce Meyer Ministries has some input as well.

John Ray's video was aired and then Jennifer interviewed me about my ministry and life in UK churches. As a parting comment, she said that if I wanted, she was sure they could find a slot for me to air my own TV programme. I was not so much motivated by the thought of being a TV personality, but it dawned on me just how many people I might reach with a television programme.

When the programme was aired, I was slotted into a prime position which came after Pastor Benny Hinn and just before the CNN News, after that is the programme with T.D. Jakes. How about that for a humble Norfolk man!

We were encouraged to add a programme that would discuss the problems that Christians have to face. Off the top of my head, I couldn't think which problems to tackle, but I wasn't going to turn down such an exciting development. I left promising to give the matter some thought.

We ate our meal and then set off for a crusade. It was well attended, and five people came forward to profess their faith in Christ. The gospel gives these people their only hope of a better life and watching them at prayer, something stirred in my heart. I am only one man and the need is great, yet there are pews full of Christians in the UK who are just as capable of sharing the Good News if they only took the opportunity.

We moved on to the Kyebando conference where over 90 churches were represented. They came from Kampala and from up-country, 283 leaders in all, plus a few extra friends! We gave them an overview of the whole Bible, all the way from Genesis to Revelation. How the Africans love to listen, how patient they are. Here in the West, we get fidgety if the sermon goes on for more than thirty minutes.

The Amin years of repression, betrayal and dreadful suffering had taken their toll on the Ugandan church. In the country as a whole, it cost an estimated 300,000 Ugandan lives and when Amin pushed the entrepreneurial Indian minority into exile, it crippled the economy. Amin's reign ended in 1979 after the Uganda-Tanzania War, in which Tanzanian forces aided by Ugandan exiles invaded the country, bankrupting themselves in the process.

Many of those pastors were still struggling with their own pain, loss and illnesses as a result of the Amin years, but when we prayed, the changes in their lives were tangible. At the end of our time together, I was moved to see these leaders in a circle holding hands, and praying for each other. I knew then what was spurring me on. Jesus could make a real difference to these people, all they needed was to hear the Good News but if I were to meet the challenge, it meant a lot more people had to be involved in a hands-on capacity.

When I came back home again, my own family was facing a different sort of challenge. My father, now aged 75 years, had been diagnosed with stomach cancer. It came as a great shock to discover that he had to have an operation in which quite a large part of his stomach had to be removed.

My mother, who was in her early seventies, was amazing. She is the sort of person, and every family seems to have one, who as the eldest in a family of five, carried the weight of everything in the family. Nonetheless, she needed love and support.

The boys were doing well. Paul was working at the Royal Courts of Justice in London, gathering information for probate cases. He commuted to London daily from our home in Lancing, sitting in the depths of a basement sifting through endless records which was all very dull until the day he came across a case involving the Premier Soccer league!

Philip was in his final year at Southampton studying for a degree in Geography. We were delighted that he was very active in the Christian Union, (a chip off the old block perhaps?) and that he had been asked to be Missionary Prayer Secretary. I couldn't help thinking that the experiences we had at home must have gone some way to shaping his desire to follow the Lord in this way. I was again reminded of my grandparents humble toilet arrangements and how God used my experiences there to help me take some of the primitive situations I have found in Africa in my stride.

My son Matthew had made very good progress since joining Worthing 6th Form college making new friends and enjoying football.

Steve now 15 years old, continued to do well at Boundstone school although he didn't actually like being there. He had worked very hard to achieve good results and he had some very close friends.

My youngest son, Jonathan in his last year at North Lancing, and

Elaine and her boys today!

surprised us all with his acting talent. We all went to see him perform and loved it.

Elaine never ceased to amaze me. She not only found time to keep all of us men in order but she still managed to find time to teach piano, and play for church worship as well as supporting me in the ministry. Life was hectic at times, but never ever dull.

1999 turned out to be a momentous year. Not only did I do four trips to Africa but I also had my first visit to Bosnia.

In the late nineties, I went to speak in Shoreham Baptist church about *Living Hope Ministries* and I met a man called John Lillywhite. Having been made redundant at the beginning of the decade, John joined Crown Agents and was working with them on overseas development. When the Bosnian crisis flared up, John, with his highflying background in industry, was the ideal man to organise the convoys laden with disaster relief. Crown Agents could be an unwieldy government organisation laden down with bureaucracy, but John became a mover and shaker, a person who did away with rules and made things happen. His involvement with the British disaster relief teams had become a twenty-four hour commitment, seven days a week.

In 1993-4 he had gone to Mostar where he saw at first hand the terrible conditions out there. The team was based in Mostar because the rest of the country was still so unsafe. The city, which sits astride the Neretva river, had been subjected to an eighteen month siege and the bridge, which had became the focal point of the city, was finally destroyed on 9th November 1993. As time went on, John became part of a team which included Dutch and Swedish aid workers, and stayed in Sarajevo until 1997, but amazingly he still can't speak the language!

By the time the programme of aid was finished, John had a real love for the people and the country and he always felt he would go back there. During this time that I went to Shoreham Baptist as part of my mission to link churches together with churches in other parts of the world. The thought of partnering with a church in Bosnia made John prick his ears up.

That first time, John and his wife Julia, went out to Bosnia where he met Zeljko and Leila from New Hope Church. The two families got on so well that they have remained firm friends ever since. Zeljko is Croatian and Leila is a converted Muslim and they have a daughter Martina. Both sets of grandparents were Serb, half German half Croat. However, they are all Christians and Zeljko's grandmother had been a church planter. Zeljko went to Prague Bible College where he and Leila met. Their church, which began in their home with a handful of people, has grown to about thirty people.

Initially Shoreham Baptist got involved to give Zeljko spiritual support. He had become very isolated in his ministry and was reliant on support from friends from Bible College and a mission from a Southern Baptist church (OVWE). They provided financial support but he needed someone to come alongside and be a personal friend. Shoreham Baptist Church's support began with prayer, and then they sent John out in person to give hands on fellowship and encouragement. He's now regarded as 'English family' and has begun to build a relationship with some of the other people in the church. Ray the church Pastor has been out to Tusla and by 2009 John was taking some of the young people there as well.

Over the years, Zeljko has been invited to England, where he has visited home groups in the Shoreham area and also the youth group. In this country, it has been said that young people don't always respect older people but when Zeljko spoke you could have heard a pin drop.

During one of his visits, John was introduced to Pastor Milos Komanovic, an experienced pastor, full of wise council and a great support to Zeljko. After hearing about *Living Hope Ministries*, he expressed the wish to be part of the LM family as well.

I began to see that practical support is vital, especially in countries where the church leaders struggle with outside forces bent on destroying the church. Who could better understand what these leaders face, than other leaders facing exactly the same thing? A germ of an idea developed into something and we introduced Zeljko and Leila to the Polish church. As a result, Zeljko is now part of a network of churches in the Balkans.

In places like the Balkans, one has to be very sensitive. You have to be very mindful of the war and the huge amount of damage it has done. Everyone has lost someone, everybody has lost property, many have lost jobs and quite a few people are suffering Post Traumatic Stress Disorder. This means that they do not function normally.

Identified in the First World War as shell shock, Post Traumatic Stress Disorder is a severe and ongoing emotional reaction which can cripple a person's life. It comes about when someone has witnessed something horrific, like the violent death of a loved one, or that person has been subjected to some sort of terror. Such sights and experiences were commonplace during the war.

I try to be very sensitive to the culture and I'm always learning the importance of dealing with these people correctly. Although the things which happened were horrific, speaking in general terms, these are a loving people.

In September I was back in Uganda and Kenya again. Travel is always quite a challenge. In places the roads looked like the far side of the moon. Potholes can be as much as a foot deep (30.48 cm.) and even with a four-wheel drive, progress is slow. Sometimes I arrived deep in the country feeling totally exhausted, but somehow found a strength and exhilaration I didn't know I possessed to preach to the people. They had probably travelled many miles themselves, perhaps walking for days to get to the meeting, so strong was their hunger for the Word of God.

This time in Western Uganda was a great opportunity and I was certainly not going to squander a minute of my time. As it was such a remote place the people were not used to visitors from the West and this was possibly the first time a conference like this had been arranged for them - even to receive Bibles, tapes and studies was very exciting. The people were so eager to hear God's word that 150 gathered - it seemed out of nowhere - to drink in everything they could. They loved question times, and it was a real challenge for me to answer their questions not knowing anything about their circumstances.

Once again, I was very concerned to be Biblical and not simply English. One big thing I dislike is colonialism. When people go into a country and do what they want to do, dictate, control and run everything the way they want it, it is in effect Christian colonialism. I was more committed to working with people and enhancing their ministries which is why at any one time an African Pastor could be running a *Living Hope Ministries* Seminar. To me, if you have a good Bible teacher, a man of God, in situ, why go to the trouble of sending someone else out there?

The aim of every trip was basically the same. I would share with the pastors and leaders during the day and in the evening, the meetings were open to all.

The journey back to Kisumu took 13 long hours with just 6 hours break in Kampala. It was hot, cramped and uncomfortable but when we arrived we were in time for the crusade. The crowd was 100-200 people, and it was such a joy to see 50 people profess faith in Christ and many testify to healing. It was good to see the whole team moving among the crowd praying and ministering. We were due to finish on the Sunday night but they urged us to go back. I was glad we did. That evening 22 professed faith in Christ, and many more testified to healing in their bodies.

The pastors' time in Kisumu had gone well, and 100 had gathered - something which didn't normally happen.

I always try to follow a pattern when I do a conference. I include a doctrine, teach from a particular book in the Bible and I leave the people with a practical application. When at the end of the conference, they express the wish for some regular training, they leave me with another challenge that I need to think through.

Bible school Kisumu

Back in Nairobi, I spent three days with the Pastors, 80 of them by the last day, which was very encouraging. By the end of my time there I had promised to send them a preaching plan to try to encourage a wider coverage of scripture. There was little consecutive teaching and although I didn't want to restrict the flow of the Holy Spirit, I felt I needed to encourage a diet which embraced the whole counsel of God.

On my last day in Kawangare I met up with Joyce Omollo again. The church there was in good heart and coming to terms with the sudden and devastating loss of their leader, her husband Joseph Omollo.

I had worked with Joseph for two or three years and he was a good friend. His home was very humble, a one room house with a curtain dividing it into two halves. He and his wife and two children slept on one side of the curtain while the other side was their living area. A big man, he had a big heart. Joseph was so committed to the teaching and he was instrumental in helping me establish *Living Hope Ministries* in Kenya. He introduced me to a number of helpful contacts and one of the things that was so touching about Joseph was that, as poor as he was, money was not a key feature in his life.

Usually, when modern missionaries return home from Third World Countries, they leave a large sum of money with the local

Pastor. Although *Living Hope Ministries* has supported the African Church financially, our main thrust has been in practical help and teaching. When I went home, Joseph was overwhelmed with people coming to him asking for money. Most people have the idea that the Muzungu (the white man) is a source of limitless money. They simply didn't believe him when he told them that I hadn't left any. It was a difficult time for Joseph and it would have been so easy for him to abandon our association but he didn't.

It came as a big shock when we had a message to say he had died of cerebral malaria. He was only in his mid-forties. Malaria is a real killer but it didn't stop some scurrilous rumours flying around. Some even said Joseph had been poisoned because people were jealous of the success God had given him. However, the new leaders, Pastor Silas from Kawangare (now the secretary of *Living Hope Ministries*, Kenya) and Pastor James from Kisumu were keen to carry on with the work.

I passed on the gifts and expressions of love I'd carried from UK to Joseph's wife Joyce and I knew it would help her to set up a small business to provide for herself and her two children, Jairus and Sharon.

Once again we gave out gifts supplied by the generosity of the people back home, distributing 160 Bibles, tapes and hundreds of studies, plus thousands of gospel leaflets and even some books in Swahili.

Back in Uganda in November, with Peter Kasozi we were able to distribute 100 Bibles, 40 New Testaments over 90 Swahili books and hundreds of Bible study notes and materials including a preaching plan and calendar for the year 2000.

Aware that the people were willing to give up everything to travel to the conferences, we asked the churches back in the UK to help us feed them. Because of their financial generosity we had the means to feed everyone who came to the conference in Arusha, Mombassa, Nairobi, Buru Buru and Soweto.

Soweto is a very poor slum. When I return home, I struggle to find the words to adequately describe the conditions that people live in. Their homes would hardly be deemed suitable for animals in the west and it always amazes me that they can keep anything dry because of the fragility of the building. Sanitation is virtually non-existent and the heat becomes very oppressive with everybody living in such close proximity. The children are far from healthy. There are no proper roads or drainage and for the most part people walk through thick mud. The one thing I cannot transport onto the page is the smell. Rotting vegetation, human and animal excreta, open sewers, flies and heat… you can just imagine the pong.

That year we had more than 300 pastors come to the conference which adds up to an awful lot of meals! It had never been my intension but *Living Hope Ministries* had gained a reputation for providing more than simply Bible teaching. I was blessed by the very large number of people who had come to be taught and trained without any thought of financial gain. I also had another surprise. Salmon's wife had given birth a day or two before and they named their little son Richard!

We stayed at the Glory Guest House, which though adequate, I am confident was a pale reflection of the glory to come!

The next two days were very useful in establishing some good relationships and laying a foundation of Bible teaching. My willingness to go off the beaten track gathered people who would never manage to go to the big centres but who were just as needy, paid off. At the end of the day three people accepted Jesus as their Saviour!

In Nairobi we saw the largest number to date at the conference when 138 pastors registered over the three days. It was very humbling to realise that each one of those pastors represented one to two hundred people.

At the crusade in Soweto, another area of extreme poverty, following the preaching of the Gospel over three nights we saw at least 30 profess faith in Christ and two deaf people said God had healed them.

I had another Peter from the UK with me on that trip. We were in Stephen's church in the morning where one professed salvation, then on to another fellowship where, unknown to me, the text and sermon were the very same as was preached the previous Sunday. A couple from that church blessed us by taking us to a very nice hotel and paying for a splendid buffet lunch. Fortunately only our luggage was weighed later at the airport, not us! My old friends at Kangemi had asked us to baptise believers in the afternoon. Peter and I baptised eight people in the YMCA swimming pool and it was a great joy to see the Holy Spirit come on some so evidently as they obeyed the command of the Lord Jesus.

Baptising people in a swimming pool was something of a luxury. People ask me if I ever worry about what's in the water when I baptise people in a river and I have to say that as always when I am on mission I am very focussed. I have baptised people in murky rivers and some unsavoury places and I suppose if something actually moved under my feet I might be worried, but usually I'm concentrating on what's happening to the person.

Rev. Peter was an active teacher of the Word and I know the brothers appreciated the variety of having two of us. This, I felt, would be a pattern which was very important for the future.

Some years later when I was on another trip, Elaine contacted me to say that Peter had died. He was about 50. Shortly after, the organ transplant people contacted her to ask for details of the trips Peter had been on with me and if he had been exposed to malaria and other dangerous diseases. It was then that I discovered that Peter had taken his own life. I really struggled with this because I knew his family and felt their pain very keenly. The manner of his death was doubly difficult to deal with because I knew he loved his family very much and talked about them all the time on our trips. Peter had been in the Falklands War (1982) and I often wondered if the depression he suffered had been as a result of the terrible things he had seen at that time.

By the end of 1999, I could see that the Lord had clearly blessed the evangelistic contribution of *Living Hope Ministries*. Now Elaine and I needed to spend time praying about how to develop it alongside the teaching and equipping of Pastors. We had come a long way since the birth of *Living Hope Ministries* in1994 but we needed to make the most of every opportunity the Lord had opened up to us.

The television programmes filmed on Saturdays had been good but as we entered into a new millennium, I decided that we should to do some filming or teaching/sharing on a Tuesday night at Lancing Tabernacle. The invitation went out to all our members and friends and they supported us well.

CHAPTER 10

The New Millennium

On July 4th 2000, I arrived at Nairobi Airport, this time with Bernard Lord. The concourse bristled with armed security people and when Bishop Stephen Kiguru met us, he told us his car had just been hijacked for the second time!

Bernard began coming on *Living Hope Ministries* trips from the year 2000 starting with Kenya. On this his first trip, he was mesmerised by the chaotic mixture of sights, sounds and smells which is Africa. He may have thought he would see hot white sands or experience the smell of wild life from the inside of a jeep on the plains but now he was seeing at first hand the open drainage systems, congested markets and throngs of people, some carrying children and/or small animals. The harsh environment of hard baked mud roads and pavements, dust and heat are made even more difficult by power cuts which can come at any time day or night. I had become used to the traffic which defies every rule in the book and the unbelievable road surfaces which resemble a recently fought over battlefield. Bernard blinked as every other driver tested the skills, the courage, the nerve as well as the patience of every one else who dared to be on the road at the same time.

I had met Bernard and Jenny Lord after they had attended a meeting in Worthing. At the time, Jenny was very ill but after the meeting they talked about both of them going to Africa on a short-term mission when she got better. For that reason, Bernard kept in touch with me but sadly, Jenny died in 1997.

By this time, I had got used to the way things are in Africa but for Bernard it came as a bit of a cultural shock to find his only shower in the B&B was standing in a bowl and pouring water over himself. At that time, electricity was a problem as well. It was off for most of the day.

Bernard was also shocked by his first impressions of the city. The people lived in tin shacks, wooden shacks or sometimes under canvas. There was rubbish and rusting vehicles all along the roads and worst of all, open drainage in deep gullies along every street. Hundreds of people milled around in the centre of Nairobi and there were few shops as we know them. Merchandise is laid out on chairs or on the ground and even raw meat hung from trees, open to the elements and the flies. At the time, Kenya was in the grip of a serious crime wave and there was a shoot to kill policy towards thieves so for him it was a bit of a baptism of fire.

In Buru Buru the planned itinerary was to be an intensive series of talks and sermons. The people were so hungry for Biblical teaching that the day usually lasted for between ten and twelve hours. We began with worship and in Africa that means rhythmic chanting, clapping singing and dancing. They can certainly teach us stuffy Englishmen something about exuberance! For the teaching sessions, I was ably supported by Bishop Stephen and by Pastor Joseph Onwudiwe.

A number of people attending the crusades came forward to profess their faith and the word of God was eagerly received, with enthusiastic anticipation and rapt attention.

On the 6th July we travelled by plane and car to the isolated village of Kisumu where a number of pastors were waiting, leaving Pastor Joseph behind to continue with the pastors and the general public assembled in Nairobi.

As I said, the day was a long one and the workload resting on my shoulders was heavy but because a man called Nicholas Wasunna and I had developed an excellent support system between us, I was freed up to preach and teach the scriptures. Nick at that time was the local representative of *Living Hope Ministries*, a man who constantly smoothed the way for us all.

We also met up with Jeff Whittington, who had been teaching carpentry skills to the men and spreading the gospel to people in the deprived areas of Nairobi. He had come to Africa on behalf of an organisation called Open Doors.

The next day, we flew to Entebbe in Uganda, where there is much more evidence of western influence with regard to its airport and its road conditions. We met up again with another local representative of *Living Hope Ministries*, Pastor Peter Kasozi who was another indispensable member of the team. He ensured that I was able to do the training and teaching programmes and sermons without hindrance.

Peter Kasozi who heads up Rock Ministries, is a very perceptive man with many fine qualities. I have referred to Peter earlier in this book. Both he and his wife, Rose, are qualified teachers and they have five children of their own. They also care for seven orphans in their own home. And if that wasn't enough, Peter and Rose run a school in a place called Kitetikka, north of Kampala. They have about 1,000 children with a very high proportion of them orphans or deprived in some way. Peter developed the school itself on land he inherited from his father. There were many disputes over the land, particularly in the lawless times of the past, but now he has built a primary school and a senior school. The school has a residential block, and about six classrooms.

Peter and Rose tread a fine line between those who can afford to pay school fees and those who are unable to pay. The troublesome years of Idi Amin and Obote resulted in many lives being lost and the subsequent AIDS epidemic destroyed even more lives. This means that there are a great many orphans with no one to care for them. Some of Peter's pupils are sponsored from the UK, but he is always in need of more.

Some of Peter's graduates are doing very well. In 1999, Anton Green and John Ray were with me when we met a photographer who, beginning with a donated second hand camera, had built up a really successful business.

Peter drove us from Kampala to Bushenyi in Western Uganda but the six hour journey was at times very arduous.

On the two occasions that we stopped for food, immediately a large crowd of men, women and children surrounded the car. They were all trying to sell us food, each trying to out do the other. We even had cooked and raw produce being pushed through the open windows.

I always try not to waste time, so as soon as I could I began to apply myself wholeheartedly to the word of God. I never regard myself as a brilliant orator but in Bushenyi over 600 Pastors and delegates listened with rapt attention and joyful enthusiasm. That has to be a work of the Holy Spirit! Their welcome towards me and the rest of the team was very warm, genuine and from the heart and they had a real hunger for the teaching of the Word. Even as I was talking, so the people continued to arrive by lorry load and as with every meeting in Africa, the praise was impressive. They sing and dance and drum giving their whole being to worshipping God.

Psalm 100 v. 4-6 *Praise him with tambourine and dancing, praise him with the strings and flute, praise him with the clash of cymbals, praise him with resounding cymbals. Let everything that has breath praise the Lord. Praise the Lord.*

Appearances are not always what they seem. We had been disappointed when permission to hold outdoor crusades had been refused but one morning, we were invited to meet with the District Administrator who explained why he had been unable to give permission. He had made his decision not out of churlishness, as we might have supposed, nor as a resistance to the Gospel He was in fact, thinking of the good of his people. A short while ago, the people in that area had discovered the horrific deaths of hundreds of cult members in an area steeped in pagan practices. The authorities were very sensitive to the mood of the people. However, once we had proved our credentials and explained who we were and why we were there, the District Administrator proved to be very friendly and wished us well in our indoor meetings.

We arrived at the meeting as usual to be greeted by hundreds of singing, clapping, stamping people. On this occasion I decided to change into the male national dress using a set of clothes that had been especially made for me in Kenya. I had admired the beautiful colours and the skilful machine stitching around the neck. As a man used to dark suits and white shirts, it felt a little strange, but the people loved it.

It was especially deeply moving to see the women coming forward to be prayed for. All of them had lost their entire immediate families, their husbands and their children. One young teenager come into one of the meetings (he had been listening outside) and asked to be saved. He was prayed for and joined us for the remainder of the meeting.

Bernard Lord prayed for people and gave his testimony. He said afterwards that to mix with such enthusiastic Christians who, despite such terrible hardship, were filled with so joy, was so touching, impressive, and very contagious. I asked Bernard to lead us in prayer at the end of the afternoon programme and follow it up with another word of testimony. He spoke very movingly about his wife and how she had longed to be with him in Africa but he also shared about how the Lord had sustained him through his bereavement.

After the meeting he was approached by female pastor, Pastor Marriet, who invited him to accompany her the next day and to speak to 40 other pastors in Dandora, one of the slums areas.

"Go for it," I told him. So the next day, Bernard set off alone, leaving me to carry on with the conference.

Dandora was a bus ride away and Bernard found himself on a bus meant for twelve with something like thirty people aboard. They got off in the middle of the market and as the only white man, he stuck out like a sore thumb. He stayed as close to Pastor Merriot as he could, terrified that she would turn a corner and he would suddenly find himself alone!

The slum areas themselves are very poor. The people live in shanties with deep culverts for sewage flowing between the houses, however the church which had been built by the people themselves, had a weekly attendance of over 500. Bernard found 40 pastors waiting for him. Once again he shared his moving testimony and talked to them about the Lord. In Bernard's own words, "The whole thing was as sweet as a pea." And the report I got from Pastor Marriet was just as enthusiastic. What other talents, I wondered, not for the first time, lie hidden and unused in the English church pew?

Throughout our time in Bushenyi, I preached on the Holy Spirit, Acts, the Gospels, Ephesians and practical pastoral issues such as church organisation and designated roles of church leaders and others. Even though it was such an intensive programme of preaching the word of God, teaching, training and advising, I tried to bring with it a level of total commitment, integrity and professionalism.

We arrived back in Kampala (the Mpererwe district), where I undertook a three-day conference for pastors and leaders with well over 2-300 people in attendance and met up with the rest of the team, Anton Green (our very efficient bookkeeper and treasurer,) Philip, my second son and his friend Mike Webb who had arrived separately in Uganda and had been gaining valuable experience at Pastor Peter Kasozi's school. In addition, we had the opportunity to listen to the very powerful preaching of Pastors Solomon, Paddy and Christopher.

Bernard Lord had taken the opportunity to go to a little school in the middle of the slums to see what Pastor Christopher was doing there with such great faith in God and a small committed team of Christian helpers.

At the end of the trip, we decided to go to a restaurant called Carnivores. They served exotic meats and Bernard sampled crocodile meat which he said was a tasty, slightly salty chicken flavour and zebra which he pronounced tough! I tasted a few meats including crocodile but overall was far less adventurous. Mick, who was part Kenyan part English, was our driver on that occasion. As we drove back to the guesthouse, we passed through an unsafe area, and a hubcap came off one of the wheels. It was imperative to get it back because Mick had borrowed the car.

"Don't get out of the car," Mick said ominously as he got out. "Lock the doors behind me."

He disappeared into the night and almost immediately people came out of nowhere and surrounded the car, trying to persuade us to wind down the windows, some in a not too friendly way.

"Don't look at them," I urged. "Look straight ahead." Bernard told me afterwards that it was the only time he's ever seen me looking really nervous.

I was.

There was an African evangelist with us in the car, a man based in London. He was a very exuberant character, larger than life and full of confidence. He thought the whole incident a huge joke but I felt we'd been protected that things hadn't escalated into something less manageable.

This man was into the prosperity gospel and he had a ring on every finger and several gold chains around his neck. He could certainly pull in the crowds but my heart sank as he held up his hands, wiggled his fingers and said, "If you become a Christian, this is what you'll get."

We left for Uganda.

CHAPTER 11

Thorny Issues

Being a teacher is always challenging and now I was faced with some very thorny issues. I felt I needed to find a way to teach the people scripture but also to allow them to practice their own culture. It was important to me that they became Christians, but of their own culture. Culture in itself is not necessarily right or wrong. I obviously didn't want to encourage anything sinful, but a lot of it was simply their way of doing things and in no way did I want them to abandon who they were.

In this country, in times past, the use of drums has been questioned. People have said that the monotony of the drum beat gives rise to a suspicion of witchcraft being involved, but no one goes as far as to say all drums in whatever capacity they are used should be banned. General William Booth borrowed popular tunes from the musical halls and gave them new lyrics, using his often quoted saying, "Why should the devil have all the good music?"

I was keen to answer their questions, bringing them back to the Bible rather than impose upon them my English way of thinking.

One of the issues the African people often raise for instance is the custom of having more than one wife. It's a massive problem. It's not just a question of whether a man should have more than one wife but what happens when a leader has more than one wife? We can look at scripture and say, "the Bible says one man one wife." But what happens if we insist that a man abandons his other wives and children? That's where you need care. Whatever the morality of one-man one wife, there's also the challenge of the physical care of the other wives and their children in a culture where women need the protection of a man.

A hardliner might argue that the first woman you marry is the legal wife. The others wives are all in effect extra-marital affairs and they have to go. Although I have no problem with that, after all it is Biblically correct, we do have to consider the other people involved. We cannot simply allow them to be abandoned in that kind of society, especially when you bear in mind that there is no welfare state, nor a social service in the way we understand it, to help people in dire straits.

I quickly realised that I had to be faithful to God's word. Whatever people's reactions, that had to be the top priority. The church had pastors and evangelists but very few teachers and scarcely no prophets or apostolic figures. My responsibility was to help them build the church with all ministries emerging and functioning.

Another problem area is dealing with witchcraft. At one time when Bernard and I were in Buru Buru in Kenya, the brothers told us that some witches would be in the meeting. They had expressed the wish to come to Christ. They told us not to worry about what might happen. Bernard was expecting only women but some of them were men. As they came to the front, they threw their amulets on the floor. Then they began screaming. A group of people were ministering to them and the service went on for ages. It was obvious that something didn't want to let go of them.

It is rare to see or hear about such demon possession in the west. I am sure it exists, but how many times have you or I seen a manifestation? In countries where people are more open to the things of the spirit, it is not unusual. Reinhard Bonnke, for instance, has a service in every one of his crusades where people who have been dealing with or dabbling in the occult are invited to come and destroy their amulets and fetishes by fire. An old oil drum is provided and once the things have all gone up in flames, the people celebrate their new found freedom in Christ by dancing around the fire.

Another time, I was having some terrible dreams at night. I was standing in a landscape. It was very flat, like a chessboard, and I could see nothing around me. Thick menacing clouds raced through the sky towards me but just as they reached me, they vanished. I tossed and turned in the bed but found it very difficult to sleep. When I got up in the morning I asked Bernard, who was on the same trip with me, how he had slept.

"I had a very bad night," he said. "I was plagued with bad dreams."

When we compared notes, our dreams were almost identical. We prayed about the situation straight away because we felt very much under attack. It would have been easy to turn back and not carry on with our mission, but the scripture tells us in James 4 v. 7 *Resist the devil, and he will flee from you.*

We saw some very disturbing things in Rwanda mainly as a result of curses. We came across a group of women who were praying for a young girl. The top of her scalp was burned away because someone had cursed her with a fire devil. It's difficult for us in the west to believe this kind of thing but her scalp had started to bubble and the women were trying to combat the curse through prayer.

On a more positive side, we saw a woman who, as a result of a curse, had been heavily pregnant for two years without giving birth. She couldn't afford to go to the doctor so she had been going to witchdoctors instead. We prayed for her the day before we went home, and by the time we got to the airport, we had a phone call to say she had given birth to a healthy baby boy.

A young man called Innocent began going to a witchdoctor about a skin complaint. The witchdoctor told him the way to get cured was to sleep with as many women as he could. He did this and eventually became HIV positive. He was with some friends when miraculously he had a vision of Christ although his friends rather like the companions of apostle Paul on the road to Damascus, could see nothing. A Christian helped him turn away from his lifestyle and witchcraft and he began life as a Christian but he still hung on to his amulets and the animal skins he put around his bed. Eventually he found total release through Christ and he was so thankful he gave up one meal a day and took it to the hospital. But the need was great and Innocent couldn't help more than a few at a time. Many of the patients don't have relations and if there is no one to bring food into the hospital, quite simply, they don't get fed.

Innocent used to be a chef so he went around the restaurants collecting unwanted or unused food. After cooking it, he took it to the HIV ward in the general hospital for the patients. Later on, the team from Elim Worthing gave him £50 from the revolving fund to help him buy larger pots and pans so that he could cook larger amounts of food. The team knew full well that Innocent wouldn't be able to pay back his £50 but they were happy with that.

This story has a very happy ending. When Innocent wanted to get married, he sought advice from Bishop Augustine Gakwaya who said he could marry if he could find someone who was already HIV positive. Innocent has now married and he and his wife have two little children who, amazingly, are completely untainted by their parents' disease.

A lot of people in Rwanda have been delivered from the effects of the genocide and now at last, both Hutus and Tutsis are worshipping together in the church at Kigali. It's an ongoing healing for both sides. The Rwandans say themselves that they let the devil run amok among them when in 1994 the genocide was in full swing. What other explanation is there for neighbours hacking neighbours to death, the slaughter of little children and the mutilation of many hundreds of fellow countrymen and women?

A young woman came to Bishop Augustine saying she had been cursed. When he looked at her arms, there was something moving up and down under her skin.

"Give me your hand," said Augustine.

"No Pastor, I can't," she said. "Whatever this is will be passed onto you." But Bishop Augustine insisted that the woman put her hands in his. Eventually she was persuaded. "As I prayed," Bishop Augustine explained, "I saw whatever it was move down her arm and as soon as it reached my hands, it disappeared."

In Nigeria, near Minna, I met an elder of the village who was involved in witchcraft. He was able to transport himself into his mud hut even though it had no doors and no windows. If I told an African about that, he wouldn't flinch but Westerners find it hard to believe. They would never accuse me of lying but they would be easily persuaded that I had asked them to suspend their belief when listening to that kind of story. The scary thing is, it's all real. The Good News is even better. Jesus came to set people free.

When Peter Kasozi was planting a church in Busiki, a witch doctor came to him and told him, "If you plant a church here, you will be struck dead by lightning."

Peter went on to plant the church regardless but the witch doctor became sick and took to his bed for several months.

I remember being in Bushinee, and as we were all having breakfast I struck up a conversation with a man.

"What is it that stops you from becoming a Christian?" I asked.

"My parents are involved in witchcraft," he said. "If I became a Christian, they would get the witchdoctor to curse me."

Umm, that was a difficult one. "If the witch doctor died," I said, "would he have any power over you?"

"No," said the man. "Of course not. Once he's dead he's gone."

"Well, Jesus died and rose from the dead," I said. "So He's bigger than anybody whether they are alive or dead!"

The man's face lit up and he was ready to receive Christ.

In Nigeria, the witch doctors are so powerful that they even know when Christians are coming over in a plane but the Bible says, *Greater is he that is in you, than he that is in the world.* 1 John 4 v. 4

I shared the word of God and we went up to the little church overlooking the village. Other Christians had been involved in praying for the work of God to be expanded in the area, including Bishop Bitrus Kato. I encouraged them not to be afraid and four people gave their lives to God.

Sometimes when dealing with the darker side of life, the situation can bring a sense of fear but at other times it's more of a sense of weariness and the need to be cautious. The more open people are about witchcraft, the more they talk about it, the more vulnerable they become. A society which opens itself to this soon finds it is overwhelmed.

When confronted with a very strong spiritual threat I usually speak in tongues, albeit under my breath, and plead the Blood of Jesus. What do I mean by this? In the Old Testament the people of Israel were encouraged to put the blood of a lamb over the doorposts and the lintel above the door. That in itself became a symbol of God's protection. God offered his protection on the basis that if blood had been shed, then Satan's rights and demands, which over sinful man are very powerful, are nullified. Where blood has been shed, the price has been paid. He has no rights. When we plead the Blood of Jesus, we are in fact stating Christ's victory. Without the Blood of Jesus, I am helpless, but by proclaiming His death and resurrection, I am safe.

Occasionally I sense that I have to be more aggressive in my assertions and there are other times when I go on the offensive and preach. I take the Sword of the Spirit i.e. the Word of God, the Bible, and speak the Truth.

Poverty, to my mind, is a curse, and in many of the third world countries where there are privations and great material needs, the devil is very active. People are enticed into all sorts of expressions of sinfulness, in an effort to overcome their poverty and their need to experience fulfilment. It becomes a breeding ground for some very suspect behaviour. Disobedience and rebellion, are, according to the Bible, a sign of witchcraft.

To end on a more positive note, a very significant part of my story as a Christian and indeed *Living Hope Ministries* has been the prophetic. At a number of key points, a timely word has come and often the immediate impact brings joy. However later, maybe sometimes years later, something said has yet more impact and fulfilment. A good example is the word brought to me in the USA. The immediate blessing was the description of "working in the dark". How amazingly well it described my feelings and thoughts as I struggled in the early days with the decision to make me redundant!

However, when a number of young men were coming across my path in several nations, that same prophecy spoke of me raising up Timothys. It was several years after those words that I suddenly saw that was exactly what God was doing. Praise the Lord! So what is prophecy today? It is a gift of the Holy Spirit and brings the Rhema word of God. It never contradicts scripture but it releases the heart of God to our spirit, to know what God is saying right now! This prophetic word is spoken and always should be tested.

There is no need to precede it with "THUS SAITH THE LORD", if it is the Lord it will come to pass. It is good to know something of the walk with God that the one offering the word is sharing.

However it is remarkable that sometimes, someone still an infant in Christ, has heard from Him. Sometimes people are given pictures or visions. We say "a picture paints a thousand words." As people wait on God sometimes a picture comes to mind and then an interpretation of what God wants to say through the picture follows. Paul said in 1 Corinthians 14 that it is good to desire spiritual gifts and prophecy. That's great! However a true prophet is not just a speaker but also a good listener.

The sacrifice of shutting oneself away to wait on God is costly but the fruit of speaking truth, which releases and builds up encouraging God's people, is wonderful. Sometimes a word of warning and caution seems deflating but when we obey, it results in health.

CHAPTER 12

Twinning Churches

I have met some wonderful people on this journey. They may not be kingpins in the Kingdom but they have been God's gift to me.

I first met Andrew Fadoju around 1995/6. He was assistant Pastor at Worthing Elim and I was the pastor of a local church in Lancing. Andrew was born in Stepney, London, but he was brought up in Nigeria.

Andrew was aware of challenges in ministry for me and when he heard about the changes I was facing, he had his own views but was extremely supportive and sympathetic to me.

Alongside his then senior pastor, David Cottrell, Andrew gave me the opportunity to help with some of the church Bible teaching courses. These went really well and helped to restore my confidence. I had felt more than a little beaten up by past events, but the call to be a missionary took more shape through these good friends.

However, shortly afterwards, David Cottrell stepped down from leadership of Elim Church and Andrew took over. We got to know each other a little better. Because Andrew is from Nigeria, (he went back there to live when he was three years old after his father died), he has a good understanding of cultural differences. I would go to him for advice, asking for an African perspective on things.

Andrew often prayed with me before a trip and many times God gave him a clear prophetic word which so encouraged and prepared me for the days ahead.

Andrew likes the fact that I have a very good understanding of the Old Testament. I may not be a dynamic charismatic speaker but so often with them it's all about their personality and not about the plain truth. I don't go in for fancy illustrations. I simply preach the

Word. If you're looking for the truth from God's word, then I will lay it out for you.

During our conversations, we took note of the fact that the gospel is about God's love for humanity. It's not English or American. For example, when the English celebrate Christmas, we may send a card with a picture of a church with snow on it. To someone living in Africa, that would be a nonsense. A picture of a person receiving a nice bowl of rice would have more meaning to the African.

From 2005 Elim Christian Fellowship, started sending out teams to Rwanda. Andrew says, "We, as a fellowship, don't live and

breathe Rwanda but it has become an integral part of what we do. Of course, the team itself is totally focussed on their calling and as a result we have raised money for a pineapple field so that the income would get people jobs and revenue to the church out there.

Augustine (far right) Rwanda

Other projects include an orphans' fund, and buying a minibus."

Don't you just love it when God takes your humble seed and multiplies it in ways you never even dreamed was possible? I do!

Andrew fells that being a part of *Living Hope Ministries* has been a real benefit to his church. The very fact that they can be a resource to another church and being able to give has been wonderful and one day he hopes to be able to invite the young people in Rwanda into closer relationships with the young people here in the UK.

Through the contact with *Living Hope Ministries*, Andrew Fadoju has made personal contact with Bishop Augustine. In fact, when he was in the UK, Augustine preached at Elim Christian Fellowship!

Even though he's a Nigerian himself, Andrew doesn't always trust African ministers. "All too often," he says, "there is a mind-set which says 'Let's find a church in the West and they will give us money.' The whole fellowship thing becomes little more than a money-making exercise."

Having said that, Andrew was really impressed by Bishop Augustine.

"The man is genuine," Andrew says. "And he loves the gospel. He's not into building his own little empire. The stuff we've given them money to do, they've done. He's honest and trustworthy."

Augustine Gakwaya is a widower with six children, Esther, Ruth, David, Daniel, Joshua and Deborah. He lives in Kigali, Rwanda. Augustine has good relationships with many Christian groups and is a member of the Evangelical Alliance. He has also served as the Vice President of that organisation. His friendship with Bernard Lord has remained firm and because Bernard is a widower himself, he was a great help to Augustine when he lost his wife, Teddy. "We say all the right things," Augustine said to Bernard at the time, "we show our concern but we never really know what it's like until it happens to us personally."

I have been concerned that Augustine might be pressured into re-marriage. The culture in Africa dictates that a man should have a wife at all costs.

Back in 1993 the Apostles and Prophets Church was registered in Uganda and came under Augustine's leadership. When he moved to Kigali, just after the genocide, he registered the church there. There are now 24 churches in this group. I met Augustine Gakwaya, before he became a bishop, in Uganda in 1997, and I have visited Rwanda since 1998. Since that time, he has become a bishop. In 2002, I invited him to co-ordinate *Living Hope Ministries* activities in Rwanda. A trusted and intelligent colleague, Augustine is a real ambassador for Christ. He has 92 churches in Uganda as well as the work in Rwanda and he has contacts in Burundi and Congo. He acts as the linkman for *Living*

Hope Ministries in all of these countries. This makes more meaning to the sense of team with brothers in Africa as well as those who help *Living Hope Ministries* from the UK.

This has been my aim all along. Facilitating people to be 'church' with one another. It's my job to preach the Word of God, hold Pastors' Seminars, provide a monthly Bible Study, send teams to far-flung places, make radio and TV programmes, keep the prayer network going and work with the churches in the UK. From time to time, other people come alongside me. They run with me for a while and then sense God's calling in another area. That's all to the good. I love that because it means the gospel message is going even further than I ever envisaged. I have seen too many great works for God being stifled or choked because the person with the original vision has been unable to allow someone else to run alongside them. It's a bit like gardening. A plant will grow until it fills the pot it's in. Restrict it to the pot and it eventually withers. As it expands, so the gardener takes shoots and cutting or splits the plant into two pots. That way, the plant goes on and on growing. I never want to keep this work all to myself. My hands alone are far too small. This is God's work, His calling.

Andrew Fadoju sits on The *Living Hope Ministries* Council of Reference which meets two or three times a year. Others include, Reverends Andrew Edwards, Graham Jefferson, John Woods, Peter Light, Ray Orr, Rev. Dr Sam Larbie and Pastor Kay Owolabi. They take a look at what I'm doing, check it against the aims of the ministry and ask the question, "Do these two things marry together?" The council of reference doesn't tell me what to do but they have become a check and a balance for me. I know that it's important to them that they care for me too. They make sure I don't take on so much that I fall into the danger of burning myself out. In fact, John Woods, the pastor of Lancing Tabernacle has given *Living Hope Ministries* a room within the church. Elaine always says that John and I complement each other. We are also good friends and John and I went to Burundi in 2010, adding another country to the growing list of places where *Living Hope Ministries* has contact.

Graham Jefferson is another member of the council who has had a strong influence in my life. I met him at a Christian celebration at the Assembly Hall Worthing where a group of ministers were praying before a meeting. Graham felt prompted to pray for me.

"God is bringing you into a new realm of authority," he said, "and into a wider ministry which will have a much greater impact than before."

I must admit I was a bit shocked but nothing more was said and we went into the meeting. A little later, I telephoned Graham and asked if he knew what was happening in my life. He hadn't a clue. This happened at the time I was being made redundant from Grace Church. Without having any knowledge of this, Graham had given me a very significant prophecy.

As for Elaine... everyone agrees that she is one in a million. She supports the work of *Living Hope Ministries*, and me (!) totally. She doesn't seek fame and even through her own struggles (Elaine has suffered from depression) she's remained totally committed to the work. In fact, I am sure that when she gets to heaven, she will have a much bigger reward than she gives herself credit for!

People might say, "I don't agree with your faith but I can see that you live what you believe." That's the kind of life I want to live. The church tries to be glamorous like the world but the world doesn't want a church like that. They want to be part of something different.

It's great to leave people with a new horizon. Since we've met, Andrew Fadoju harbours a desire to go to one of the Eastern European countries. He says his reasons are personal but I know that he has the feeling that people don't really warm to black people and he would feel more challenged to go and meet with Christians in Eastern Europe than if he came with me to Africa.

"Why take me to Africa?" he chuckles. "My face would just fit in with all the rest!"

So as well the Worthing Elim link it's been encouraging to see Shoreham Baptist Church come alongside Zeljko and Leila of New Hope Church in Bosnia. Lancing Tab has links with New Life Church and Pastor Jeremie in Burundi. Toddington Baptist Church is twinned with Word of Life Church in Kisumu and East Grinstead New Life Church has connections with Philadelphia Church in Romania. Mitcham Elim prays for Emmanuel in Sierra Leone and Sompting Christian Fellowship is linked with Bishop Stephen in Kenya.

Not all the churches are from the affluent West. The Balkan churches support Pastor Isaac's work in the Congo. Added to that, a number of individuals across several churches sponsor children in Peter Kasozi's school through *Living Hope Ministries*.

It seems to me that we become more like one big 'family' every day. Jesus never promised to build my ministry but He did promise to build his church. I am totally committed to building church and make it a major teaching subject wherever I go.

CHAPTER 13

New Horizons

David Fordham used to live in Guildford but his Mum lived in Goring. She worshipped in the United Reformed Church and David went with her one night to hear me preach. I don't think even he knows why he came up to me after the meeting but something about my setting off on my first trip to Africa with only one name and one telephone number in my hand struck a chord with him.

David had been thinking about being involved in a charity but he found himself on the horns of a dilemma. He was deeply distrustful of the people who run charities. He was aware that some organisers actually waste charity funds, and so becoming involved with one wasn't something David was about to take on lightly.

"I'm interested in the work of *Living Hope Ministries*," he told me, "but before I go any further, I would like to meet you in your own home."

It was an odd request but I had no problem with that. What I didn't know was that David expected to find me living in a plush house, with a big car. What he found was an ordinary house on an ordinary estate. Elaine and I have never been extravagant. We live modestly and any funds I receive for the countries where I serve, goes there, not into my pocket.

After our meeting I was delighted to learn that David felt strongly that *Living Hope Ministries* was a charity he could work with.

Soon after he got involved in the charity, David came out to Africa with me. When he came back, I invited him to join the trustees. The board at that time was Peter Lewis, Ray Butler, Mike Radley, Jim McIntosh and Val Secord. He was so impressed by the other trustees that David is now the Chair. He says "It's a blessing and privilege. In actual fact, we sit in the meetings with Christ as Chair and Leader and when we've weighed all the different projects and plans, we take it to God in prayer. As soon as we feel we know what He wants us to do, we step forward into that, almost always without the money to achieve it! That's never a problem because I have seen time and again how the Lord provides, pretty much to the very penny".

When on his trip to Africa with me, David found it fascinating that no matter what went on around us, I somehow managed to maintain a sense of calm. I'd never really thought about it but there have been so many times when flights have been delayed or cancelled or we've not had the money at the end of the trip to pay the hotel bill and it seems as if everything is going to go pear-shaped. What is the point of panicking? I have found that every time I take it to the Lord in prayer, the prayer is answered immediately and the money arrives to pay the bill or we can make alternative arrangements. We are on the Lord's business anyway.

David continues to work in the secular field but seeks to bring his skills into the work of *Living Hope Ministries* wherever he can.

After the Polish trip, the Board of Trustees discussed the physical implications of me going on every single trip. I had to agree with them that the workload was indeed becoming far too large for me to carry alone. As we talked and prayed we decided that some teams were quite capable of going without me.

When Paul Newett joined as administrator it took a huge load off my shoulders, and when my daughter-in-law, Charlene Brunton joined as my PA, the same thing happened. But as we took on more training of Pastors, more time had to be given over to writing courses and studies. Having more people doing the courses, so that I didn't have to write everything myself, would be a tremendous help.

In May 2002 I took a small team over to Poland. Our flight from Heathrow had been a smooth and uneventful prelude to what was to be an exciting, busy and productive four days. The plane landed at Warsaw Airport where Pastor Andrzej Nedzusiak was waiting to welcome us and take us to our accommodation.

We were actually looked after by another church organisation in an area of Warsaw called Praga, and from the outset of our visit we were warned that the town had a very high crime area. It was noticeable that every apartment block window, door and shopfront was protected by metal bars and heavy metal doors were fitted over the normal doors.

The main city roads in Warsaw are very wide and straight, which allows a relatively small volume of private vehicles (compared to London) to move at break-neck speed around the city. Who says the Christian life is without excitement!

As we drove to our accommodation, we noticed that in some places you could put your hand between the bullet holes on the brickwork.

The Pastors have to break down age-old prejudices. It's hard trying to persuade the older people to own their own Bibles because for so long the religious leaders forbad Bible reading. Thankfully, the younger generation don't have the same hang-ups.

We came across a church which was held in a derelict building. It had once been a house but the only access was through a front room. There was no staircase and the upper floors were wrecked. Everybody sat on benches against the walls on the ground floor. The church had suffered a great deal of opposition and even during our meeting there was some disruption. The meeting numbered fifteen people (the result of the prayers of just two people) and what they lacked in numbers they certainly made up for in their commitment, attentiveness and in the vocal strength of their praise. As usual we could only join in with one or two songs. The language may differ but the tunes are the same. Considering the intimidation they had previously suffered, nothing was hidden from those passing 'the shop window' and everyone sang lustily.

When we talked with the Pastor and some of his people after the service we discovered that they all had a strong sense of evangelism and purpose. Amazingly, these people go out twice a week, every week to give out tracts and evangelise their area. They also spend one day a week ministering to the homeless. John 13 v. 35 *By this all men will know that you are my disciples, if you love one another.*

The Pastor went outside and a few minutes later he came in with a man. I could see that the members of the congregation were surprised to see the newcomer but he sat still and listened intently.

We later found out that this man was the main instigator of all their problems. He had even been violent towards the members, but that day God had convicted him. He had knocked on the door, not to cause trouble, but to apologise and to ask to come in. At the end of the service, he committed his life to Jesus. When the service ended, the 'shop front' had its steel doors closed to give the place complete protection.

Warsaw, is the ninth largest city in the EU and the capital city of Poland and straddles the banks of the Vistula River. Known as the Phoenix city, Warsaw was extensively damaged during the Second World War. It is renowned for its fabulous palaces and churches, and yet a quarter of Warsaw is made up of many small neighbourhood parks, areas of green space, courtyards, and tree-lined avenues. Ruled after 1945 by the Communists, the people remained staunchly Catholic and the Polish Pope John Paul 11 was received with joy when he came back to his native country in 1979 and 1983.

"Let Thy Spirit descend!" he cried at the end of his sermon. "Let Thy Spirit descend and renew the face of the land!" As we were about to discover, the Lord heard and was already answering that prayer.

Wherever I go in the world, our hosts always want visitors to be aware of their particular country's deepest wounds. One man, Andrzej was no exception. He took us to see the memorial dedicated to the Warsaw Uprising, a 63 day struggle to liberate the city from Nazi occupation. It was very moving.

Later that day, we travelled to Kutno about 100 kilometres from Warsaw, to a church with the wonderful name of Christian *Jesus is Alive.* The number of worshippers was small, but once again we were overwhelmed by the praise and worship and the commitment of the people. After the service one of the ladies invited us back to her home for a meal. The generosity and friendliness of the people were very impressive, moving and so very genuine. It's a great honour to be there and I love ministering to such people.

Later that evening, we set out on an hour's drive to our next destination, a place called Skierniewice where we had been booked into an hotel, which must have been quite a financial outgoing for such a small, relatively poor group of people.

The day in Skierniewice was a full teaching day for Pastors and Leaders and was held in the home of one of the ministers, where fourteen people were in attendance. I began by sharing my testimony and talking a little about the way the Lord has led me into other countries.

The sessions were based around 1 Samuel and I talked about God's plan to bring the tribes together under David and to exist as a nation.

- God's plan to build leaders up and for them to lead by example.
- The testing of leaders.
- Hearing from God.
- How we hear from God.
- The church as a place of discipleship and not just converts.

I enabled the pastors and leaders to exchange ideas and to ask questions.

They prayed for each other and offered each other moral and spiritual support.

Day four of the visit we were back in Warsaw, in Andrzej's church. They meet in a local, general-purpose community hall, rented to Pastor Andrzej every Sunday morning for worship.

We received a very warm welcome from the 150+ people attending the service.

It was interesting to note that the children sat in child-size chairs at the front of the church and joined in the worship. Some of their praise songs had a very dramatic Slavic lilt, whist the others were easily recognisable as the same songs as we sing in our own churches.

The church has a School of Prophecy, in which the people are encouraged to develop their gift, and at one point in the meeting, someone came up to us and prophesied over us. Tired but contented, I had the privilege of praying for a couple of people before going to bed.

Sunday afternoon and evening were spent in Sochaczew, a 12th century town 50 kilometres from Warsaw. Rebuilt after the destruction of the war, Sochaczew has lost a lot of its original beauty, but fortunately there is little serious crime.

The service was held in a very run-down, very small three roomed house. After a year, this house has now been given official recognition to be able to conduct services, which is a welcome relief, as the local community and the authorities had been very hostile towards them in the past.

At one point in our service we had been praying that local difficulties would be overcome when a man walked into the room. Immediately one of the brothers got up and the newcomer was led out. It transpired that he was one of the people who had been continually opposing the church, but on this occasion the man had come in to tell the Pastor that he no longer objected to the premises being used as a church!

Bernard Lord said afterwards that his visit to this little church was one of the most uplifting moments for him in the whole of the Poland trip. The Pastor, through sheer determination and faith, carried on every day, fighting local community and official hostility, and he was winning the battle.

Until Pastor Andrzej had received his calling there had been no Christian church in Sochaczew. He started with two or three people and no accommodation, but after knocking on doors as well as bill posting around the town, he has slowly gained acceptance and recognition. He has ten or twelve regular worshippers every week. I very much felt that I should be a 'Barnabas' (a son of encouragement) in such circumstances. How humbling to experience the warmth and eagerness of these people as visitors to their church.

The praise and worship was very heartfelt and uplifting. Anybody passing by in the street couldn't help being aware that this was a house of God.

I was delighted to hear that once again, a married couple for whom I had prayed for the year before, had been given an answer to their prayers. They were now the proud parents of a healthy and very lively baby boy. After the service they invited us back to their home. We were treated to a beautiful meal and I was aware that they must have spent a great deal of time and money on its preparation, probably something which they could not easily afford. Their home, although warm and friendly, was little more than an outbuilding or shack. They told me warmly that I was now a part of their family. Praise the Lord!

Back in the church, I felt it right to teach from the Word in a way in which was relevant to the trials and difficult circumstances that this small group of dedicated Christians were experiencing. I told them Jesus did not live in a palace. You can meet with Jesus anywhere, whether it's in an African hut or in a small room in Poland.

At the end of the service people gathered for prayer. No one missed out on the opportunity, not even the small children who had grouped themselves around the door leading into the room. The visit also gave me opportunity to give some advice to the young Pastor on how he should handle one of his Elders who was proving to be a disruptive influence in the church.

Later we were invited to have breakfast with an elderly lady who attended Pastor Andrzej's church. Her late husband had been a

Pastor himself and on more than one occasion had been imprisoned by the Communist authorities for his faith. Despite their threats, the Pastor would not stop preaching and he repeatedly held baptismal services in his own bathroom.

We chuckled as he recalled an incident when the police went as far as putting locks on their home so that he could not carry out his illegal activities. The Pastor tore the police locks off the door and took them down to the police station telling the police what he had done and that they had better put him back in prison. But by now, they were so fed up with him, they told him to go home and not to bother them again. His faith had won the day. I had opportunity to pray for his widow and also to give some 'fatherly' advice to the young Pastor who was struggling with one of his Elders who was proving to be a disruptive influence in the church.

That visit to Poland proved to be a highly successful and productive time for all concerned and we were able to distribute various literature, clothing and even some knitted teddy bears!

Later on in the year, in August, I set out for Eastern Europe with Bernard Lord again. This time we went to Bosnia.

In March 1992, Muslims and Croats living in Bosnia, fearing a drive for a Greater Serbia, called for a referendum for Bosnian independence. This was followed by some fierce propaganda from Serbia in which the Muslims were depicted as extremist fundamentalists. As a result, many Bosnian Serbs supported Milosevic's plan for ethnic cleansing.

Bosnian Serbs began a siege of Sarajevo on April 6, 1992. Residents opposed to a Greater Serbia were denied access to food supplies, utilities, and communication. Through three long, cold winters, Sarajevans lived in constant danger from sniper fire as they collected firewood and tried to get to their jobs. The average weight-loss per person was more than 30 pounds and by the time the war had ended, more than 12,000 residents had been killed, 1,500 of them children. Now that *Living Hope Ministries* had a foothold in the country, we were determined to keep going in order to build the church up and to encourage the brethren.

Our flight had been a smooth and uneventful one. We changed planes at Zurich in Switzerland for the flight to Sarajevo in

The church at Tuzla

Bosnia. At Sarajevo, Pastor Dusko, whose church we were visiting, drove us to his hometown of Tuzla approximately 140 kilometres from the airport.

The airport was quite small but busy and as well as Bosnian police and airport security officers, we saw members of the UN peacekeeping force in place. It was a little disconcerting when people standing just a few feet away from

you were being led away by the security police! We could also hear quite heated arguments going on between returning passengers and police. It seemed that the mood and attitude of those in authority at the airport was cold and even slightly hostile with no smile or words of welcome, quite unlike the trip that Bernard and I had made to Poland in May.

On the journey to Tuzla, the beauty of the landscape was breathtaking. A cloudless deep blue sky and brilliant light served to enhance the dramatic, scenic views of the rugged slopes and forests that curved up to meet the mountain tops as well as the panoramic views of the deep valleys. The wooded slopes of the mountainside were liberally dotted with houses all along the route to Tuzla, which at times was reminiscent of the two or three storied homes that are built on the slopes of Switzerland. However, that is where the similarity ends.

Many houses were nothing more than burnt-out shells, heaps of rubble. Those that remained were scarred with the marks of heavy gun and shellfire. Paradoxically, all along the route we saw a great many half-finished houses, but no sign of men working on them. Apparently that was because people built until the money for materials ran out, but they still made the building a home. Consequently, people were living in houses without upper floors or windows, or doors and in some cases without a front or a sidewall or even a roof!

After a three-hour drive, we arrived in Tuzla. It was 5.30pm and at 6.00 pm I began my programme of preaching and testimony to a small gathering of about fourteen people. The Church, Tuzla Baptist Church, was on the first floor of a dilapidated, three storey building in a room approximately 20ft by 15ft. The room was spartan, with cracked and peeling walls. Two adjoining rooms of similar dimensions served as the living quarters for Pastor Dusko and his wife. They had lost their home and possessions during the time of fighting and ethnic cleansing.

Initially, when the pastor and his wife approached the authorities asking for permission to start their own church, the request was turned down. The only reason that they were allowed to have a church after the end of the war in1995 was because they threatened to go to the American President, Bill Clinton who was himself a Baptist.

The authorities, not wanting at the time to sour relations with the Americans so soon after cessation of the war, granted permission, hence the name Tuzla Baptist Church. Those people who had managed to attend the meeting received us warmly.

I remember particularly the evening service with its praise songs, one of which was Amazing Grace, sung in a melodious manner, quite beautiful and touching in its intensity.

As Pastor Dusko read from Philippians 1:1-11 without any prompting, everyone present, out of their deep respect for the Bible, stood up in their traditional way.

I remember that my theme for the duration of that visit was building God's Church, and of His guidance, designs and plans for His people. I laid emphasis on God's love, His suffering and His

Son, our Saviour. The terrible events that had turned Croat against Bosnian, Christian against Muslim in their recent war and ethnic cleansing was not a deterrent to those attending that particular church. There was a mixture of Croats and Bosnians, even some who had a Muslim background. One such girl asked for healing on her marked and bruised arms, the result of her being beaten every time she attended church.

The Church was not able to afford food or refreshment, so we provided enough money to allow the Pastor's wife to slip out for some bottled water and food for everyone attending.

The Sunday service had by far the biggest attendance, with more than forty people. It was touching to hear the congregation singing, Blessed is the Name of the Lord. They sang it every Sunday especially for a little Down's Syndrome child, three or four years old, who clearly loved it. Everyone, middle aged and the elderly alike, did the actions energetically. To me this was Love in action.

The war has left people terribly emotionally scarred. Leila herself has an amazing story of God's deliverance. As an ex-Muslim, she was one of the people who were taken away in a lorry. Everyone knew what would happen. Like so many others before them they would be taken to forest areas where they would be made to get out. A short distance away, they would face an open grave where they would be shot and buried. Leila had been first on the truck, so she, heavily pregnant with her daughter Martina, was right at the back. The soldiers stopped the truck and ordered everyone off.

Leila had been praying, "Lord don't let this happen."

Everybody else got out but she stayed where she was. A guard came back, looked inside, opened the curtain at the side of the truck and called to his comrades, "They're all out." Leila was still standing in the truck as large as life and yet he didn't see her. As soon as they'd all gone, she got out and escaped.

I preached on the person of Jesus, His powers and abilities, His patience and love bringing in the way Jesus always referred to

"The Father." I was able to relate the Bible to their circumstances in a way that they could understand. I also gave them plenty of opportunity to ask questions as the people became more relaxed and responsive.

After the sermon I invited people to come forward for healing. It wasn't surprising that I ended up ministering to a people damaged by hatred, bigotry and violence. Everyone there had a terrible story of personal loss, albeit of family and friends or of torture and intimidation, but thank God, Jesus is the Healer!

It's incredible how God is creating a whole *Living Hope Ministries* 'family'. Bernard has talked to Zeljko and Leila from Bosnia about his experiences in the Congo. The Congo is desperately poor and in fact, the rebel army was only a few miles from the place where the team was staying. After the team had left, the rebel army came in and killed a lot of local people.

Bernard's enthusiasm, together with *Living Hope Ministries'* Africa links have inspired Zeljko and Leila to support work in the Congo themselves. They have asked him to go Bosnia and talk about the Congo and show the photographs of his trips.

Bernard raises his own money to go on these trips. He doesn't ask anyone for help. He is a retired Head of Department from Northbrook College and a very popular art teacher. He chose to give up his job to look after his wife, Jenny, during her final illness and when she died, he wondered how he was going to manage. He uses money from teaching adults how to paint, to fund his airfares and accommodation and he is generous with his giving to the people wherever he goes.

It seems that God has given me a veritable army of unsung heroes.

CHAPTER 14

The Power of Prayer

Being on the mission field is not always plain-sailing. I have a great many stories about disasters and troubles, but the one redeeming factor is always that the Lord is in control. We can look back with laughter on so many incidences.

Baptisms are a case in point. Sometimes people coming up out of the waters have such a wonderful experience, I am sure that they have seen the Lord in person. I recall one lady who immediately spoke in tongues but there have been others that I have had to hang on to for fear that in their ecstasy they would go under again and perhaps never come back up!

I also recall being in Kampala at the dead of night. I was taken to a very poor area to preach and I was delighted to find about 100 people in the church. However, my excitement was short-lived because in his introduction the pastor said, "We have a real man of God here today. I know he must be a man of God because no-one else would come to preach here at this hour." That should have made me feel very important but then he went on to describe the area as full of drug addicts, prostitutes and how no one in their right mind would even venture to be there. It was even a no-go area for the police. By now I was feeling far from the man of God he was portraying. In fact, I was inwardly praying, "Help Lord, what have you got me into? How am I going to get out of here?"

Another time I had been invited to preach in the west of Kenya. The Pastor was unable to get transport for that night so we had to travel the next day. I had nowhere to stay, having already booked out of my guesthouse accommodation. Undeterred, the Pastor took me to Dandora, a very poor slum area where I was to stay the night before setting off very early in the morning. The plan was to hire a seven seater Peugeot in order to get around to the various meetings. When we arrived at someone's house, the people there decided they wanted to pray after I went to bed.

"I'm fine," I protested. "I'll stay up and pray with you. I don't want to rest."

But they insisted that I should sleep.

When I saw the room they had prepared for me, I was really nervous. It had heavy bolts on the door and it looked more like a prison cell. It was so small, I even had to walk over the top of the bed in order to get into it! I spent a hot and uncomfortable night and what with the loud praying next door, sleep was impossible.

The next day we journeyed into the middle of nowhere and ran out of petrol.

"What are we going to do now, Lord?"

I don't know how they do it, but in Africa it happens time and time again. The driver disappeared for about twenty minutes and then reappeared out of the bush with a full petrol can! We continued the journey, with the area becoming more and more remote. Eventually, we arrived in front of three mud huts in a clearing, with perhaps a handful of people waiting. To add to my discomfort, the driver was going to leave.

"You will come back for me," I almost pleaded as he drove off.

Now I was alone and completely at the mercy of strangers but once I started preaching I felt a lot happier.

Afterwards they gave us something to eat and insisted that I rest but by now I was all fired up and raring to go.

"No, no," I said. "We've come all this way, I want to preach again."

They agreed to hold another meeting and by the time I got back into the mud hut, I was utterly amazed. About 50 people were crammed inside and waiting for me. Where had they all come from? I had absolutely no idea. It turned out to be a very powerful meeting. I gave an invitation after the sermon and about 20-30 people came forward. The noise was tremendous as people were being saved and set free from evil spirits. I had to step to one side and let the Holy Spirit do His work.

When we got back to Nairobi, I felt a little ashamed that I had been so worried, and afterwards I discovered that as a result of that meeting, new churches were planted and there was a mini revival in the area.

I'm still not overjoyed when I'm asked to go down a track and into the bush, but whenever I do, I've always found a group of people hungry for the Word of God and God does amazing things every time.

Elaine and I have always believed in the power of prayer. In fact there is nothing we like better than the times when the five boys and their partners sit around the table with us and we share together. One of the most precious times is when we pray together.

I like to think of the ministry of *Living Hope Ministries* as a great big family and so to get this wider family praying together is very important. The idea of First Friday Prayer (the day of the week is immaterial) was in order that our partners in the gospel could share things and we could all pray together. The degree to which people are involved isn't easy to measure. Here in Lancing, we have a meeting and several faithful people come each time to join with those who can come as and when they are able.

Some partners pray on their own, or with their immediate family, while others actually call the people of their various churches together. Peter Kasozi in Uganda, has a Prayer Night on the First Friday and any prayer requests are sent to that.

I get regular feedback from people like Bishop Augustine Gakwaya in Rwanda, so he's obviously praying or getting people to pray. Stephen Kiguru prays and Brother R in Pakistan prays with his family as well as calling a leadership meeting on that day. In India, SJ Kumar also prays on First Friday.

The First Friday prayer meeting and the monthly Bible study go hand in hand. For obvious reasons, it's not always wise to publish every prayer request in detail, but it is an opportunity to remember people connected with *Living Hope Ministries* and the study will help to spiritually feed them.

Some people encouraged me to go to the USA as a source of funding. It is well known that American Christians are extraordinarily generous but I really didn't want to make that my sole reason for going to the States.

My early visits to America were assisted by others and it was noticeable that when I had opportunity to minister, I was sent to very poor areas. The people there needed help and were in no position to give to us. It seemed to emphasise all the more that my ministry is to the poor and the needy, quite the opposite to going to the States for money! And I feel quite comfortable with that. In one church in Chicago I was told it wasn't unusual for people in the area to be shot. This only served to reinforce my conviction that these were the kind of people God had called me to, not the affluent and the well-to-do.

My last trip to America was linked to my contact with Brother R in Pakistan. For safety's sake, I cannot reveal his name. Brother R and I had first come across each other via the Internet. As time went on, we talked on the telephone and prayed together. When I went out to Pakistan to meet him it was a real step of faith. We'd never met face to face but I simply put my trust in God.

Brother R's brother had met an American girl on the Internet and they got married. I didn't realise at the time but the girl had been married before and had a child. Both of them had embarked on a marriage without knowing each other very well and as a result they were facing huge challenges.

However, when I went out to the States, I was hoping to use some contacts I had been given to raise money for another brother back in Pakistan. At first he did seem to have some good contacts but sadly in the first church we went to, the Pastor was having some personal family problems and he felt he had to step down from his ministry. We got on well and I liked him but once again, a door I thought might useful only opened far enough for me to be able to offer some comfort and pastoral care to someone in need. Having said all that, I am open to a return visit.

On my first visit to Pakistan, it became apparent that Brother R was ministering to people but he had not been ordained. Although some might have thought of me as being presumptuous, I felt it was important to recognise what God was doing. Thus on our first meeting we set aside a time of prayer and 'sent him out'.

Brother R came from a completely non-Christian background but his family, his parents and his brothers, have all come into faith and we had the joy of baptising his father while we were there. If you look on the website, you will see that all references to Pakistan have been removed. This is because Brother R and his family live in an area of the country which is very hostile to the Christian message. We would not put anything in the public domain which might endanger his life, the lives of his team or the lives of the people in his church. It is for this reason that we never mention the actual locations in Pakistan.

On my first trip, I was introduced to a Christian policeman. He had a loaded rifle and a necklace of bullets. He was there to protect me. As I went to bed, the policeman went onto the roof and during the night, I could hear him moving around. At one point I heard a sound outside and someone tried my bedroom door. A scary moment.

"Who's there?" I called nervously.

Thankfully it was only my 'protector' checking to see if the door was locked.

Even the meetings themselves were challenging. I couldn't help thinking what the tabloid press might make of someone sitting at the back with a rifle. I can imagine the lurid headlines. *British Pastor gets converts at gunpoint.* Or perhaps *Be a Christian or be shot!*

We thought it best for people to travel to me rather than for me to move around but at the last meeting, we were faced with a situation where the people attending the meeting had to be scanned for bombs or weapons before they were allowed inside. As we spoke, three armed guards patrolled the roof for any troublemakers.

If this sounds scary for us, Brother R's wife has accepted the fact that her husband is constantly moving around dangerous areas and what little resources they have, have been ploughed into God's work.

One can still have meetings in Pakistan. In some places they gather in their hundreds, but on the whole, people meet in their homes.

Brother R took me to the home of a lady at midnight. She had been beaten by people hostile to the gospel and her son was in prison on trumped-up charges. Brother R encouraged me to share the gospel. The man of the house came in and the couple's daughters were there. At the end of sharing I gave them an opportunity to respond and I felt the Spirit of God was moving. They all had their eyes closed so each person had no idea what the rest of the family were doing. Every one of them gave their lives to Christ and a couple of days later, we baptised them all. On a subsequent visit I met the whole family again and they are still following Christ.

At one time, another of Brother R's brothers was put in prison. We prayed for his release and he had a vision of me coming to his cell and comforting him. We had no idea how he could possibly be released. We had to leave that with God. The people who had made the false allegation against him went to the police. "We're very sorry," they said. "We made a mistake. This man didn't do it." The authorities still took a while to sort it out but happily the brother was released.

Another time, Brother R took me to a meeting. A lady sat in front of me wearing a purple scarf. As I watched her through the meeting, it was like watching a flower opening up. It reminded me so much of Lydia in Acts 16 where the Lord opened her heart. It's great and yet so humbling to have had experiences that seem to come right out of the Bible's pages.

After the Tsunami there was some concern that the money sent to Pakistan wasn't getting to the people it was intended for. When the earthquake happened in Pakistan in 2005, it was centred near the city of Muzaffarabad. It happened on 8th of October and measured 7.6 on the Richter scale. To put this into some kind of perspective, it was equalled to the 1906 earthquake which hit San Francisco. The official death toll in Pakistan was 79,000. The destruction was immense. *Living Hope Ministries* collected more than £10,000 which for us was a large sum of money. Brother R had never handled money on this kind of scale before. I trusted him implicitly, but for his own protection, we sent the money in smaller portions. He was amazing. He bought clothes, tents, and food, and in one place he set up a Living Hope 'village'.

We found out later that some Pakistanis living in Britain were personally taking the money they had raised out to the stricken areas because they didn't trust the authorities to get it to the people who desperately needed it. Brother R didn't put a foot wrong.

Brother R has Hepatitis C. For a full healing, he needs a miracle. We are praying for him and asking God for that miracle.

Another person who benefited from prayer and practical Christianity was an African lady called Agnes. Even though she couldn't speak a word of English, she was an amazingly inspirational woman. Agnes had lost almost her whole family through the Rwandan genocide and illness and at one time she was looking after fifteen orphaned children. Agnes never complained about her hard life, on the contrary, the team from Worthing Elim Christian Fellowship remember hearing her testimony and almost every sentence was prefaced with the word "Halleluiah!"

Her conversion to Christ came about when Bishop Augustine was asked to pray for her sister who had recently died. He went to the sister's hut explaining that all he could do at this late stage was to commend the lady to God. However, when he got there, although everyone was wailing and crying, he felt strongly that the deceased should be prayed for in a sitting position. He persuaded the people to haul her up into a sitting position and as he prayed, she began to jerk and came back to life. Agnes became a Christian that very day.

A recipient of the Revolving Fund, Agnes used her £50 to buy charcoal, which she would bag up and sell to her neighbours, but life was still difficult. One of the children in her care broke his arm. Agnes could afford to pay for the arm to be set, but not for aftercare and the arm became infected. The team from Elim Christian Fellowship were anxious to help.

"It'll cost a lot of money," said Bishop Augustine. "It cannot be done."

"How much money?" Bernard asked. He was mentally thinking of some vast sum and of how he would be able to raise it.

"Thirty pounds," came the reply.

Needless to say, the team paid for the treatment and thankfully that young boy is fit and healthy.

In 2008 Agnes went back to her own ancestral village. She had cancer and she wanted to die among her own people. She left an indelible mark on the lives of everyone in the Elim team for her courage, hard work and her love for God.

The positive way in which Worthing Elim Christian Fellowship had made possible such schemes as the pineapple field and other forms of help e.g. the purchase of a generator, Bibles, and the Orphans' Fund and the Widows' Fund has been a blessing to our African friends and brothers. Bernard told me that although they were grateful for what the team had been able to do for them, what they didn't realise was how much they have given the team in return. The team had been spiritually fed and they had seen some wonderful examples of Christian inspiration, commitment and devotion.

'I can do no great things, only small things with great love.'
(A Coptic Christian).

I make a point of praying about emails that I get. A man called Johnny De Vila emailed me to ask for programmes to air.

Pastor Johnny is a team leader for Mutual Faith Reality TV in the southern Philippines. Founded by Keith Hershey with his wife, Heidi, Mutual Faith Ministries International works in several countries, including Ghana and West Africa where they have saved twenty women from Trokosi (a form of slavery) in the Volta region. They set up homes for impoverished children and give them an education and food. Keith Hershey has also written and published numerous books, and hosts the weekly television programme, LIFE Unlimited, airing in over 120 nations.

Johnny didn't ask me for money which would have been difficult for *Living Hope Ministries* to find, so we sent a couple of programmes. After a month, he emailed me again to say, "We love the programmes. We are putting them on every day, please send more!"

David and Carole couldn't possibly manage three hundred and sixty five but we have managed to send enough to air one a week.

In 2009, David and Claire Richards went to the Philippines where they visited "General Santos City " in the Southern Philippines. Their hosts were none other than Pastors Johnny and Josephine De Vila. They discovered that the network runs 24 hours /seven days a week and also runs a counseling service. Both Pastors have their own TV programmes and the station is broadcast locally and includes the hospital wards. Johnny and Josephine also run the Life Leadership Institute, with the expressed aim of equipping and training new disciples and church members. Their church is called Word of Life Cornerstone church and they have just finished building a multi-purpose building at the back of the church.

David and Claire went to help to teach and train the students and to be part of the Graduation service at the end of the week. They quickly established a great rapport with the students and were able to give them prophetic words of encouragement. The Graduation service itself was to herald the commissioning of sixteen workers into the harvest field.

Our God answers prayer!

CHAPTER 15

Yet More Countries On Board

So how did some of these other countries become a part of *Living Hope Ministries*? I guess the answer to that question is mainly through networking. For instance, Stephen Kiguru invited me to Tanzania. Rwanda came about after I met Bishop Augustine. At the time of the genocide, some Rwandans fled to Uganda and Augustine was one of them. He didn't sit around brooding about his plight, he became salt and light where he was and now he's got more churches in Uganda than he has in Rwanda.

Augustine came to a conference at Kyebando. I was very impressed by this tall, elegant man. I had begun to take some good Christian resources out with me. Things like The Lion Handbook of the Bible, Bible Commentaries and dictionaries, etc. I had discovered that Christian Literature Crusade would let me have these books at about a third of the price if I gave them to the developing world. I had one big Bible Commentary left and I was praying, "Lord, to whom should I give it?" I saw Augustine and walked across to give it to him.

Augustine took it in his hands as if were holding a precious jewel and said, "Lord, thank you for this gift for Rwanda."

I held my breath in as he thanked God that his nation would be blessed by a book, which speaks volumes about the selflessness with which these men give their lives for their country and for the gospel. We struck up a friendship which is still going strong to this day.

Nigeria came about in a totally different way. Some friends who were supporting me in the UK, Graham and Hilary Collins, knew a Nigerian called Nat. They invited him to a *Living Hope Ministries* meeting. In the early days of *Living Hope Ministries* I did a series of Saturdays going through a book of the Bible or a Bible character like Moses, or David. We were doing a video and Nat came over to tell me that he had a friend in Nigeria called Bitrus Kato who had access to the local television station.

I got in touch with him and we began to share our programmes. Eventually, after about two years of sending the programmes, I went to Nigeria to meet Bitrus. As soon as I saw his face after the very long journey by air and road, I knew instinctively by God's Spirit that he was the right man to work with. Time and time again I found I had to literally make a journey of faith and then discover that God had prepared the right person. It was also true of Brother R in Pakistan and Emmanuel in Sierra Leone. .

Bishop Bitrus Kato died in 2008. He and I had worked together for several years and I appreciated so much his enthusiasm and energy to make Christ known. He chose to work in the more difficult and challenging parts of Nigeria and he wasn't afraid to go to other countries where there was fierce opposition to the gospel.

The television ministry we shared was so fruitful and I will never forget making a programme with him in Minna, and then seeing it a few hours later on the TV in his office. Almost as soon as the programme had finished his mobile phone was buzzing with people wanting his help. Thoroughly devoted to his wife Sister Betty and his family, Bitrus was such a thoughtful man, and a constant encouragement to me. He frequently sent me a greeting or an exhortation to press on and believe God had more for me to do.

The last time I saw him in Nigeria he actually paid for me to stay in a very nice hotel while he took more humble accommodation. As if that wasn't enough, he arrived at my hotel early enough the following morning to get me to the airport on time for my return to the UK.

Bitrus was not only a great servant of God but also a powerful role model emerging leaders with his participation in the wider Africa team. He understood my purpose and vision so well and made every effort to support me. Above all he was our friend and we are all the poorer without that friendship. His concern for

Elaine and his patience and love for the two of our boys he met, (Steve and Jon) was so special. I remember fondly how he cared for Elaine and Jon in Nairobi while I went on to Mombassa. I sent a tribute to his thanksgiving service which was read out in Minna, it ended with the words of Jesus "Well done good and faithful servant!"

It was 2009 before I was actually able to go to Sierra Leone. Emmanuel from Sierra Leone had got in touch with me several months before, but because of other commitments, I couldn't go for some time. I began to preach some sermons over the mobile. The people would listen as it was translated and Emmanuel kept emailing me to tell me of the positive response to what I was saying. The reports were so glowing I felt I had to go and see for myself. Either God was doing something very remarkable, or the reports had been wildly exaggerated.

I went with Christopher Lane from Norfolk, and right from the start it felt as if we were getting some right royal treatment. Emmanuel had even sent a senior police officer to escort us through immigration.

The journey from the airport was certainly eventful. Coming over the estuary by ferry took a very long time and when we arrived at his house, Emmanuel insisted that we had his bedroom, which meant that he had to sleep on the floor in the next room. We were both moved by his generosity, even more so when we realised that Emmanuel had suffered a break-in just a few days before we had come. He had very little furniture left, but even then he gave the best of what he had to us.

Emmanuel has certainly known more than his fair share of suffering. In 2008 his wife, Princess, a young woman only in her twenties, died very suddenly and he has been left with a baby son to bring up on his own. His mother-in-law helps him but it's poignant to know that Junior will never know his mother.

Emmanuel has founded a school called Vision Preparatory Primary School, and we began our visit by meeting the children and the staff. A hundred and ninety two miles, and five hours later, we arrived in Kenema, where an evening crusade had been arranged. More than four hundred people attended the meeting and after one and a half hours of worship, I preached, and 50 or 60 people gave their lives to Christ. We also invited people to come for healing from depression and a release from the devil's hold on their lives. More than eighty people come forward and Chris and I were kept busy praying for them.

The pastors' conference had 150 booked in for the first day but it rose to 200 later in the week, and as it was my first time in Sierra Leone, I began with a foundational message after which a number of the delegates expressed their wish to be baptised. In fact, this was a first for us both. Emmanuel confided that we were the very first guests for whom he had arranged such meetings. After such a wonderful beginning, neither of us was disappointed.

There followed an evening crusade with 1,000 people attending, 150 of whom came forward to receive Christ for the first time. I write this sort of thing so many times in my reports back to the trustees and supporters of *Living Hope Ministries* but I never tire of it. *Jesus Christ is the same yesterday and today and forever!* Hebrews 13 v. 8

Then there were healings. A small boy with poor vision in his right eye, a man with pains in his side… so many needs but we brought them to a Jesus who is the answer to every prayer.

The next day at the conference I told them a bit about my life, the birth of *Living Hope Ministries* and its ongoing mission. Then we put faith into action. The people prayed with us for Chris Lane, for the wider work of *Living Hope Ministries*, especially the work of Brother R in Pakistan, and for the future work that may be possible in Sierra Leone.

We had managed to take a lot of literature, including a revised *Living Hope Ministries* Pastors' handbook - a book that was printed for me some years ago in India - and many Christian classics. We made a point of buying books locally as the Lord had given us favour with a Christian bookshop in Freetown. We managed to get them at a very reasonable price. It not only saves shipping costs, or having to pay excess baggage charges at the airport, but it also supports the local Christian bookshop.

Sadly, one of the evening crusades was rained off, but it didn't stop us enjoying some very good fellowship with Pastors Jesse and Emmanuel, and by the end of our time there, the total of new converts had risen to about 350.

On Sunday, we had a very early start, as we went to Star radio. This is not a Christian station but a Christian slot had been made available for us. After starting with a brief for a 15 minute talk, a note was passed to me saying we could have another 15 minutes, doubling the time to 30! We left there with a wonderful offer that we could share a 30 minute slot each Sunday - 15 minutes of LHM radio and 15 minutes from Emmanuel.

Pastor Charles, who has a prison ministry, invited us to go with him into the prisons. Prison in Sierra Leone is a far cry from the prisons in the UK. Here we saw 179 men milling around in a secure compound, with cells around the edge. The smell was awful.

We went into a small cell, in the heart of the prison, where one of the prisoners led the worship. I preached about the thief on the cross. Had I known that there were men in the prison who were under the death sentence, I probably would never have chosen that particular text. After a gospel message, seven men gave their lives to Christ. As we left, someone handed me a piece of paper on which he had written, "I have been in here since 2002. I have had no trial. Please pray for me." Thank the Lord, several of those men have now been released, including the worship leader. We then moved to the neighbouring women's prison but we were told that there was no way we could preach there. When we arrived, we came across women with little babies. I had no message prepared and so I was surprised when one of the warders said, "You can preach." I chose the story of the woman caught in the act of adultery which again, had I had time to think about it, I might not have chosen. My message was not a condemning one. I chose to emphasise the fact that Christ said, "Go and sin no more." Five ladies gave their lives to Christ and I later discovered that some of my 'congregation' were actually in there because they had killed their husbands because they had found them with another woman!

Some people have picked up on the fact that I am not always aware of what is going on around me, but these two stories show how God has used this very trait in a powerful way.

Returning to the airport was a lot easier because we went across the estuary in a small boat powered by an outboard motor. It was a bit scary when, halfway across the engine cut out, but it soon spluttered back to life. The boat stopped about four metres short of the shore, but a very eager group of men carried all our possessions and us ashore, so we arrived on dry land looking rather like modern versions of Victorian missionaries!

Contacts come from just about anywhere. Rhoda from Worthing Tab was getting letters from someone in Malawi so she suggested that we go there. I went to see her Pastor, Mark Weeden and a few months later Mark and I went to Malawi together.

Sudan opened up because we unofficially adopted Wandii, who was part of Bishop Stephen's church. Stephen also initiated our becoming involved in the Congo.

Sometimes, things don't work out so well but the Lord overrules. They introduce me to others where a more lasting friendship develops. One man moved mainly around London and one of the churches we went to was Rev. Major Sam Larbie's church at Camberwell. As time went on there were some problems and the relationship between this brother and Sam soured. However Sam had invited me to take some meetings. When Sam questioned me closely, I had to make it clear that I was my own man in God.

Since then, Rev. Major Sam Larbie has been a fantastic blessing to us in the ministry. Sam believed in me and invested in *Living Hope Ministries* when there was nothing much to be seen. He saw by faith and as mentioned shared prophetic words, words which have come to pass. He was a great support when my wife's mother died and he has always been an encouragement. When Elaine was ill, his love and thoughtfulness were amazing. Praise the Lord!

Sam once told me, "In the office, you are quiet but in the pulpit you are strong. Richard," he said, " you preach like an African!"

It was one of the loveliest compliments I have ever been given.

Sam's invitation opened another door for me. His church was the first church to give *Living Hope Ministries* a regular donation every month.

As I have already said, Sam is gifted in prophecy and at one of his prayer meetings I went forward and he prophesied, "Resources are going to be coming to *Living Hope Ministries*, and God is opening the door to Eastern Europe."

I was a little taken aback because I had been struggling with the fact that the work I was already doing was becoming a heavy caseload. However, if that was what God wanted, and he provided the resources, that was fine by me. I would plan to go into Eastern Europe as soon as it was feasible.

That was on the Wednesday and by the Sunday I was utterly amazed to have already received £4500! That was exceptional. It was a daunting prospect but such a powerful prophecy coupled with all the money collected, I began to say, "Well Lord, it looks like you want me to go into Eastern Europe but where do I start?"

The Lord had the next part of the plan already in place. Soon after I was preaching at Bildeston and I met Chris Fox. Chris had been working in Eastern Europe for over 30 years and she had built up a great many friendships among pastors and church leaders.

She had begun with a dream in her heart and by asking the Eastern Europeans what sort of help, if any, they might need. Over and over again the reply was, 'Yes, we'd love your help but we would much prefer regular contact and real friendships and not just one-off visits'. As a result, she formed EPIC (European Partners In Christ) to be a link between the churches in the UK and the church in Eastern Europe. The churches were not simply having dialogue but 'meaningful relationships' with each other. She encouraged the UK churches not only to give money but also to get to know the people, the area, and to share in the opportunities to equip and strengthen European Christians.

Chris Fox introduced me to Zeljko which is how I got into Bosnia. She introduced me to John which is how I got into Romania and she introduced me to Andrzej which is how I got into Poland.

India came about in an entirely different way. I was asked to contact a brother who had just been made redundant by his church. I went along to encourage and pray with him. He came to some African countries with me but he also had a friend in India, so he set up the contact for *Living Hope Ministries*. This led to more relationships and ministry with another brother who has become a very good friend. Praise the Lord!

Ministry in India is a sensitive issue so few names are mentioned. Our chief contact has a great vision to reach rural pastors and his good contact with a television station has been great for LHM.

As Paul says in Romans 15 v. 20 It has always been my ambition to preach the gospel where Christ was not known, so that I would not be building on someone else's foundation.

It is good to keep that in mind.

The Pakistan connection came out of the Internet. Brother R saw the *Living Hope Ministries* website and began first to email and then to phone. I went out to Pakistan with Brian Marsh and as soon as I met Brother R I knew our meeting was of God.

Looking back, almost every contact that I've made has been a step of faith: Bitrus, Emmanuel, the Indian brothers.

Of course, I have to filter the emails, but God has graciously given me a kind of instinct about each one. I am nervous, and I never presume, but after prayerful consideration, if I have a gut feeling that the contact is a godly one, I encourage it by faith. Someone once prophesied over me that God would guide me, and that when I was on the wrong road, he would put the blocks in for me. I don't think for one minute that means that I should be irresponsible, but if there's a block, I won't go. I am so grateful for these warnings and I recognise it as a blessing from God.

It is obvious that people from the UK have been changed after they have encountered *Living Hope Ministries* but the more important question has to be, does it make any real difference to the African, the Pakistani or the Croatian?

In this day and age communication is so much easier than in the past. Emails have been an integral part of the feedback we get from the people we seek to serve. I love it when we get emails like this...

My name is Pastor Porter. We have planted 6 churches within 2 years in Benin and Togo Republic. We reach the lost and equip the saints in their search for perfection.

For some time now I have been studying the Word of God through your website Living Hope Ministries. Truly your message titled: Walking with God preached on 17th September 2006 and among others pierced through my soul and blessed my Christian walk with the Lord. You have pointed me to Christ over and over, and brought more peace to my Christian life and walk with the Lord. These past weeks have been among the richest in terms of spiritual experience, teaching etc that I have very experience in my life. I was longing for a closer relationship with God my Father. Through your Internet teachings, my desire has become a reality.

This particular pastor went on to say that his people were up against preachers who only want money, give new age messages and perform fake miracles. Some of his fellow ministers have even resorted to using occult powers and witchcraft in order to have bigger congregations! My calling has been to make the gospel clear and because I have always resolved to preach only Christ, people like Pastor Porter have been blessed. To God be the glory!

In 2003 we received an amazing email from a lady called Grace Semwogerere. Again, I have reproduced it as she wrote it.

The kind of happiness I have cannot be clearly described. True I have much to say about what happened to me which I never experienced in my life. On 25th when you were praying in your compound and my eyes were on the small screen of my television (it was my first time to view programmes on LTV) I was hit by a force I couldn't resist which made me to land on the ground and started babbling like a baby. When I got up, none of the family members could tell what had happened to me. Good enough my neighbour is a born again Christian and when I told him about my issue, he told me that the force which striked me was the power of the Holy Spirit. Lastly he asked me if I was willing to surrender my life to Jesus Christ. At last I had to accept and he prayed for me. Today I am born again Christian. He is now my brother in Christ and I request you to accept to be my spiritual father. I am a Ugandan aged 38.

Only a couple of examples, but they speak for themselves. I also reproduced an email sent as recently as 2009 from India. (This is exactly as it was written.)

Dearly beloved brother Richard ,

Greetins in the name of our saviour Jesus Christ.

We are still recalling the memories we spent with you.

Thanks for your gift toward Internet charges.

Rakshna TV says that they have more than 1 billion viewers.

It is telecosted in diffrent countries where Telugu speaking people are more.

It is 24 hours Christian telecasting channel.

Our programme comes at every last Sunday at 7 am. for 30 minutes. comparatively this channel has wider range and less money.

They are telling me in the telephone that if we have weekly programme they will repeat the programme whenever they have free time. So each programme is repeated at least twice a week for which we do not need to pay anything.

I am giving some reports through telephone:

"We worship god only on Friday as it is holiday in Kuwait so we don't get time to go to church on Sundays. We are blessed with your programme "Living Hope". We watch at 7 am on Sundays. This is a convenient time as our owners will not wake by that time. So we are learning God's word that way. Why dont you have programmes each week?" Laxman – Kuwait

"There are so many programmes in the TV now a days…but yours is wonderful programme to learn the word…why dont you have your programmes each week?" Seeta – Dubai

"We pray God to bless your programme as it is enlightening our understanding of the word of God I wish you have more programmes in TV" Balakrishan – teacher

CHAPTER 16

Family ties

My daughter-in-law Charlene Brunton who is married to my fourth son, Steve, tells me it is very rare to have a whole family who are all so close. All my sons are wonderful men, and I am hugely proud of them, but then I would say that wouldn't I!

My eldest son, Paul is incredibly supportive of the ministry. He works in London and gives up his time to collect visas, which is very helpful. Some embassies have got to know him quite well. Paul was only sixteen at the time of my redundancy and more aware of its repercussions than the younger boys. He is extremely loyal and even though Elaine and I did our best to protect him, inevitably he took on board some of our pain. Elaine and I forgave everybody years ago, but sometimes the way we treat each other can have a lasting effect in ways we least expect.

The other boys serve God in completely different ways. Matt is a DJ and works in the secular world. His girlfriend is called Maria and they can relate well with non-Christian people. Jon is seriously thinking about Christian ministry since his first visit to Africa with Elaine and me and Phil is a teacher, married to Julia. They are both committed to serving the Lord wherever He takes them.

Charlene moved from Belfast to Lancing in 2002. A young man from the Belfast church had taken a group from Lancing over to Belfast and Charlene became very friendly with one of the girls. As a result of that friendship, she came to Lancing for a holiday.

Charlene was all set to go to Australia for a year but waiting for the train on Lancing station she felt that she couldn't leave. She was in two minds. She had raised a lot of money to go to Australia and she didn't like Lancing, but the feeling that she should stay was very strong. Back home in Belfast, she contacted the pastor at

Lancing asking if there was a job going. Her own pastor in Belfast wasn't supportive of the change of plan but a month later she was here.

Charlene had no friends and didn't know anybody when she set foot in Lancing. She was nineteen when she became the youth leader at our church but Steve and his brothers gave her a hard time. Eventually Steve got involved in youth leadership as well and they became friends. Two years after she had arrived, Steve developed feelings for her which at first were not reciprocated. Charlene had put us all on a pedestal and because of that she hardly ever spoke to us. She regarded the family as holy, holy people.

At the same time, Charlene was going through a hard time with her family. She asked me to pray for her, and so the next day I asked her how things were. "I was so taken aback that this busy, busy man had the time for me," she told us much later on, "and that he cared enough to find out."

When she first started going out with Steve, Charlene came round to our house. At the time, Elaine was suffering from depression and was in bed. Charlene saw for the first time that the Bruntons weren't 'holy' in the way in which she was thinking. They were an ordinary family with the same trials and joys as everyone else.

When Charlene and Steve got married, I really wanted to take the wedding ceremony myself but the young couple had other ideas. I suppose I was a little hurt at first, but I can see the wisdom of it now. It was a chance for me to be there for Steve simply as his Dad. Anyway, all was not lost. I was in my element when they asked me to preach the sermon!

Charlene went to great lengths to include us all in the preparations fo their wedding. She and Elaine made the invitations together, and Elaine and I were able to go to Belfast for the day to meet her parents. Charlene, her mother and Elaine went together to collect her wedding dress and of course, a few tears were shed when the mums saw her in her dress.

After they'd been married for some time, Steve worked on Saturday at a garden centre and Charlene was left on her own. She began to pray, "Lord, what do you want me to do with my Saturdays?" She felt God saying, "I want you to give them to *Living Hope Ministries*." At first, she wasn't keen. She knew I worked a seven day week and she didn't want to be caught up in that sort of work ethic. As an elder of the church and her father in law it was a privilege to have Charlene seek out my counsel and help. After a lot of prayer a new door of service opened up for her. She now works for *Living Hope Ministries* for two and half days a week. Someone donated some money for her wage and a prophecy from my old friend Sam Larbie in London, confirmed what was happening. She now works as my Personal Assistant, sending letters out, doing my diary and helping to plan the trips etc.

Balancing my family life and my ministry has always been a priority. As you can imagine, the demands on my time are enormous but it's important not to pay lip service to the needs of my family. We are very close and it seems hardly a month goes by without a family gathering. It always seems to be somebody's birthday or celebration, and I must say I am in my element when we are all together. Elaine and I were married at 21 and 23 years. We went straight into ministry so we can see our lives reflected in Charlene and Steve's ministry.

Steve came out to Nigeria, Uganda, Kenya and Rwanda in 2003 when he was nineteen and in 2005 he came with me to Poland. The experience wasn't to his taste but he was careful not to say, "Never again!" People loved Steve's frank and honest

Opening a Bible school in Uganda with Charlene and Steve

reports of trips on mission. He obviously saw God's hand but found some challenges.

Since then he and Charlene have come with me to Uganda and were greatly used by the Lord.

Steve wanted to work as a full-time worship leader. He began as youth worker and enjoyed it. He has always had a feeling God may call him to be a pastor but he is anxious to find his own identity, rather than be considered as Richard Brunton Jr. Worship is really important to Steve. For him, worship is far more than simply singing songs.

The year 2002 was momentous in more ways than one. At the age of 79, and having survived stomach cancer, my father had a fall. I was due to go to Africa on the Tuesday. By Saturday he still hadn't regained consciousness and things started to take on a much more serious note. He had a series of mini-strokes and we were faced with the prospect this time that he might die. As time went on, I had to consider, do I go on this trip or not? As the weekend progressed it was obvious that things were taking a down-turn.

Matthew 10 v. 37 became incredibly real to me. *Anyone who loves his father or mother more than me is not worthy of me...*

After talking with the family, my mother, my brother, Elaine and the boys, I decided that, whatever happened, I should go on the trip. My father died on Tuesday morning and I left on Tuesday afternoon. I shall always remember in particular the way all my sons stood with me on that day. They stood as one man to support me. The Lord gave me the peace that surpasses all understanding. Everything around me was not peaceful but as I flew up over Heathrow I had a wonderful peace. I was doing the right thing.

The thing that is most important about the fifteen years of *Living Hope Ministries* is that there is virtually nothing that isn't wholly 'Elaine and I'. We are more united on this we have been on anything else. This doesn't mean that I should negate any of our private time together, but being as one in the work, has made an enormous difference. I have made a big effort to ensure that this ministry is known as the ministry of Richard and Elaine. When a husband is busy doing one thing and his wife is busy with something else, it can create tensions in the family. We decide things together. I've never been on a trip where Elaine isn't happy for me to go. I remember once when she was unwell, I seriously thought I would have to cancel a trip. I expected her to say, "I want you here," but instead she insisted that I should do the trip.

Elaine is the one who always writes a note of thanks to those who give a gift to *Living Hope Ministries*, but since the boys have grown older she has been freed up to be more actively involved. Most Sunday lunches we have the family around the table, and we also enjoy walking together. My favourite route is along Lancing seafront, a reasonably unspoiled stretch of beach, where the winds are bracing.

Elaine started travelling with me to the various countries in 2006. We went to Poland together. She actually loved meeting the people who up until that time had been just names on a report.

When we were in Uganda together, Elaine was put into situations which she may not have chosen, but she took it all in her stride.

I have to be careful not to put a square peg in a round hole but there is a place for everybody. If I'm in a situation where I think someone is not doing a thing well, I try not to simply take it away from them but rather to find a way of putting something in its place. Change should never be a negative thing. I was left with nothing so I know how hard it can be.

CHAPTER 17

People I've Met Along the Way

I want to pause for a moment to recount some of the people I have met along the way. Some of them have already gone to heaven and I will always be very grateful for their help and encouragement.

I was once on my way to Fakenham to take a meeting when I felt the Lord say to me, "You're going to meet someone who will help you in the ministry."

At the end of the meeting Matthew and Chris Wright came up to me. They were actually in the area visiting Chris' parents, who lived some distance away but they had felt compelled to worship that Sunday in Fakenham Baptist Church. Matthew and Chris had a burden for Uganda and we talked about it. He was the pastor of an Assemblies of God (AOG) church in Alsager near Stoke-on-Trent, Staffordshire, England and I asked him, "Who's preaching in your church this Sunday?" It turned out to be Geoff Richardson, a previous pastor of an Elim church in Brighton, a man whom I knew very well. Remembering what the Lord had said to me I was getting the feeling that something was coming together.

Just after that meeting with Matthew and Chris, I was invited to be interviewed on Revelation TV. When I got there, instead of talking about the ministry as I expected, they asked me to talk about baptism. After the programme I received a great many calls - one of which came from someone in Liverpool who said they would love to be baptised but the church they attended didn't believe in baptism by total immersion. They asked me if I knew of someone who might baptise them and the only person I could think of was Matthew.

Since then, our friendship has grown from strength to strength. It was really good that in 2010 we were on a trip together. Matthew and Chris's contribution is very valuable and although parted by distance it's great to have them as part of the *Living Hope Ministries* family.

I have already briefly mentioned Nick Wasunna. He is a six foot five Anglo-Kenyan who lives in Nairobi. He offered John Obayo practical help with his sewing co-operative when a flood of second-hand clothes knocked the stuffing out of the Kenya textile industry. John tends to be very generous and didn't always charge people for using the facility. Nick helped him apply some sound business principles and the operation has now reorganised to do alterations and to teach people tailoring skills for a small fee.

We met up in the Namirembe guesthouse in Kampala, high on the hill overlooking the Anglican cathedral. It was close to the place where, in 1977, Archbishop Janani Luwum was murdered. Archbishop Luwum had vigorously protested against arbitrary killings and unexplained disappearances. Amin accused him of treason by planning to stage a coup. In February 1977, Luwum was arrested together with Erinayo Oryema and Charles Ofumbi. The next day, Ugandan radio announced that all three had been killed when the car taking them to an interrogation centre had been involved in a collision but when Luwum's body was released to his relatives, it was riddled with bullets. There were rumours that Amin himself had pulled the trigger although he always angrily denied the charge.

Looking out over Kampala, it was with a full heart that I reflected just how much this wonderful nation had achieved since those dark days. Nick told us there was far less corruption.

Nick's testimony is a wonderful story of God at work. He was always a really wild young man. While he was in college in England he had two main passions, rugby and getting drunk. He sobered up when he was seriously injured after being hit by a car. After his recovery, Nick's father sent him to work in the bush. To everyone's amazement, he was converted to Christianity in a tiny mud hut, way out in the sticks. He is now employed by World Vision and the considerable energy and talent he gave *Living Hope*

Ministries is now helping them greatly. ... a big man with a big heart.

Trevor Bond is an old friend, (Elaine and his wife, also called Elaine, were both bridesmaids to each other at our respective weddings) and in 2005 he gave a prophecy over my life.

"I saw a billet of red-hot steel being run into a rolling mill for shaping. It went through a succession of shaping rollers until the form was that of a steel joist. The Lord says that he has taken you through the furnace of adversity and then a shaping process that, with each challenge, has made you more fitted to your designed role. As an RSJ is not seen that much but is a vital part of the support and stability of the building, so he has made you increasingly ready to carry the weight of the support of others in fulfilling the task, making it possible for the building that he is constructing to be erected."

Looking back and remembering that prophecy about the three doors given to me all those years ago by Trisha McCarthy, it took my breath away. As the hymn writer says, "How good is the God we adore..."

Julie Shimizu is another person the Lord has used in a prophetic way to speak into my life. She once prophesied, "'I will make you like my signet ring, for I have chosen you, declares the Lord Almighty.' It seems to me,' she went on, 'that God is using you to put your mark or seal on places like on a letter or a parcel. You aren't actually going with the parcel but you are leaving a mark and sending it off.

Haggai 2 v. 23 *'On that day,' declares the Lord Almighty, 'I will take you, my servant Zerubbabel son of Shealtiel,' declares the Lord, 'and I will make you like my signet ring, for I have chosen you,' declares the Lord Almighty.*

The Lord says, 'This is a time that many new doors will open. You will be the one to open the doors but you will not be alone. Those who accompany you will be the ones who go and come back through the doors. You will in practice, spend more time at home receiving reports, envisioning and encouraging those who come and go.'

Emanuel Rubenbana pastors a very large church under Bishop Augustine. I came into contact with him in 2001 when I went to Rwanda.

He was nervous and inexperienced but all that he and the other African brothers needed was the confidence to rely on the Lord and to trust in Him. The church in Rwanda has benefited in many ways through *Living Hope Ministries* and those who have a greater vision for the country. Rubenbana is also generous in his praise. "For sure," he explains, "the ministry has carried us a lot. People had no money. We could not get power to hold the activities in the evening. Then the *Living Hope Ministries* teams came in and they contributed different things. One team gave us a generator which really helped us to hold services in the evening." Rubenbana used to have a little workshop but increasingly he felt that he should trust in the Lord and branch out into full-time ministry. Bishop Augustine encouraged him and now he runs the Apostles and Prophets Church in Kigali.

"Before I worked with Augustine full-time," he says, "the Lord sent me to a place where I established a church. It now has 100 people, and we still disciple the people who lead that church."

Rubenbana is keen to serve *Living Hope Ministries* International because he has a passion to reach out to the rest of the world. He feels that God has blessed his country and the Apostles and Prophets Church in Kigali.

"If you are blessed," says Rubenbana, "you also ought to bless this people you are blessed by."

Another man who has had a strong influence on my life is Rev. Graham Jefferson of New Life Church Durrington. He was the pastor who, back in the nineties, prayed for me and gave me an encouraging prophecy.

Graham has given me moral support more than anything else. We regard each other as friends, and Graham is on the Council of

Reference. We offer each other encouragement, support and guidance.

"It's been great watching a little acorn grow into a mighty oak," Graham says. "I don't think anyone is more surprised at what's happened than Richard himself. He has grown in confidence and authority over the years. He is highly honoured because he is so different from the Western itinerate minister the Africans in particular have become used to. There is no razzmatazz, no five star hotel and driving around in a limo. Richard is a man who identifies himself with the people."

Several pastors and ministers in Worthing meet every Tuesday morning for prayer and encouragement, and I have been part of that for many years. We began with a discipleship course, and we still study together. It has been somewhere where we can talk over problems in confidence. Some of these men wouldn't be in ministry today if it wasn't for that group.

I cannot finish this chapter without talking in some depth about Bishop Augustine Gakwaya. As I have already mentioned, I first met him in a meeting in Kampala Uganda about eleven years ago at a meeting under Denis Haywin.

What follows next is Augustine's impressions of the work of *Living Hope Ministries* as he sees it.

'Richard was a meek minister in the way that he came and identified himself with us. He was a person who could show love, feel loss and desired to know more about each individual at the conference. What I saw was very impressive. He could easily identify with the local pastor and he loved us and from that time he deserved to come to Rwanda. We had a great time at the conference.'

Since that time, I have organised ten or more conferences in Rwanda, as well as attending other conferences in Uganda, Kenya, in Cornwall (UK).

The contribution LH has made for us, can be best summed up by saying, the teaching given by LH has enlightened, uplifting knowledge, wisdom. We have also had different teachers from UK and other African regions especially Kenya. He came with a lot of materials, including Bibles, which helped a lot of Pastors. We also had a computer which we use to show the Jesus film and so many other selected books. He has also has opened doors for a Rwandan church like mine to meet other ministers from different parts of Africa like Nigeria, Tanzania, Kenya, Uganda as well as connecting us with UK church such as Elim Church in Worthing. They have been such a blessing to us and the teams have visited us about five times. They have contributed towards us in way in which we are weak in terms of our finances and transport. They have raised money for a pineapple field, selling and buying homes for the destitute ministers. It's not only giving us material things, it's also been about building friendships. It also involves prayer networking which we do every first Friday of the month. We are a big team worldwide.

The Elim church from Worthing come for ten days at a time and go out helping the needy, uplifting students and helping students to acquire higher learning in a Bible college. We are about to acquire our first degree holding teacher in our ministry all of which comes about through the generosity of the Elim church.

It has been a blessing to meet a good man like Richard and working with LH is getting a blessing beyond your expectation.

Normal day. Simple live full of grace and triumph. We survived all our calamities including the genocide in 1959-60 and the one in 1994 simply because of Jesus Christ and speaking of Him who brings hope to the hopeless.

I have a big day every day. The big work involves 26 churches in Rwanda and 100 in Uganda. I have meetings, problems to sort out and on top of that, we have series of meetings involving me negotiating for our church with the government. I also have a big family to attend being a single parent. I have to invest a lot of time to my children. I normally have a busy day and I need your prayers!

The churches in Rwanda have people with different and unique problems. The uniqueness is because during the genocides of 1959-60, a series of killings in 1963 and 1973 as well as the 1994 genocide, left people handicapped. The mothers died, the fathers (the bread-winner) died and so people are handicapped. Even those who have a chance of learning *and get good jobs, are still handicapped. We are attending to many orphans and widows. But our church has been a blessing to others and whenever the Elim team come they say these people are a blessing to them.*

Our church is a new church, 15 years old but we try our level best to live as the New Testament church in the Bible and by the grace of God, take Rwanda for Jesus.

Things are improving in Rwanda. Tony Blair came as an advisor for the president. He has done a tremendous work and what he has done will benefit the country and give us a great future. The authorities are beginning to put systems in place which mean that people can go to hospital at certain times for free consultations for minor ailments. If the people cannot afford 'proper' help, they will go to the witchdoctors and even a secular government is aware that they do more harm than good.

These things benefit the country but spiritually we still have a long way to go. We have people who are spiritually wounded and some still traumatised by the killings. We pray that the church will stand in its position and be like Jesus. They will know them by the fruits they bear."

Bishop Augustine faithfully prays for *Living Hope Ministries* when we hold our First Friday meeting every month.

"Richard is a good communicator," Augustine says. "He sends texts, emails and calls frequently. Living Hope has been a divine contact ministry. Through that ministry Elim Christian Fellowship Worthing church have come to help us. Their love and generosity really helps our church. We want Living Hope Ministries to live long and reach many nations. I enjoy investing my time and energy with Living Hope Ministries.

I say Amen to all that. To God be the Glory!

CHAPTER 18

Eastern Europe

Since those first visits to Poland and Bosnia… my how we've grown!

The European Leaders' Conference has been taking place for several years now. It is a wonderful opportunity to meet, pray and look to God for direction together. As *Living Hope Ministries* has grown, the possibility of making a personal trip to all the countries involved, Romania, Poland, Bosnia, Bulgaria, Moldova and the Ukraine every year is remote. I haven't even managed to get to Moldova as yet! However, our commitment is firstly to the people we have come to know in these places, then to their country.

Some of the people who attended the conference, Andrzej, Lola, Julian, Asa, Zeljko, Lela, Ioan, Fevi, Pepi, Nevena, Ivan, Natalah and Uri are very special servants of God and all are significant people in their nations. We enjoy excellent fellowship together and then move on to prayer and discussions about the ongoing work in the various countries.

The ministries of Andrzej (currently President of the Evangelical Alliance in Poland), is part of a movement of 50+ churches. Zeljko, works with several churches in Bosnia but also co-ordinates the work in Macedonia, Kosovo, Serbia, Croatia and Slovenia. Ioan cares for eighteen churches in Romania and Pepe looks after the Vidin church and a village church plant in Bulgaria. It is a privilege that *Living Hope Ministries* can gather such people together. We help the delegates from Eastern European countries with the cost of their travel, but it is still a great sacrifice for them. Their journeys can be very long and tiring. Ioan drove for fifteen hours!

Another key purpose of our meetings is to encourage the pastors and churches in Poland. In June 2009, we had an excellent meeting in Andrzej Braieleski's church, where one man gave his life to Christ. The time with Pastor Julian's church in Kolo was also very encouraging. The inspirational worship always blesses us and so many there are good friends. The Saturday conference with Pastors was again a valuable time and they very much appreciated hearing live reports from the other European countries, together with updates on *Living Hope Ministries* in Africa and Asia. Sunday ministry took place in several churches and Elaine and I were in Warsaw with Andrzej. This church is a testimony to the wonderful work of God. The vision and energy of the people is very encouraging and they are very blessed by Andrzej's leadership. An unexpected visit to Pastor Zion's church in Warsaw was great and again one person professed faith in Christ. The enthusiasm and love of these people was so touching and their respect for Andrzej gratifying.

The generosity of the Kolo and Warsaw churches too, was very wonderful. The Balkan churches in friendship with Zeljko are also supporting Pastor Isaac in the Congo and now our friends in Poland, Bulgaria and Romania are part of that project.

We are continually reflecting on how we can better plan and increase our effectiveness. Leila wrote to us afterwards, "It is great when we are together in Jesus. The last conference was beautiful and we believe that many good things will grow out of the seeds, which were planted during the last week. Thank you for your friendship, love and care."

Nigel and Val, two people who joined us on the trip, observed, "Earlier in the year, we had a text message from Pepe in Bulgaria, asking about the conference, saying how much he valued it, as he had no other contacts with Christian brothers and sisters. It was with joy that he was able to attend this year with his wife Nevena. We were privileged to experience the sense of friendship, fellowship and the joy of being together that our brothers and sisters from Eastern Europe feel. They were also grateful for the teaching they hear from Richard, as many do not have the privilege to hear from other speakers and have to rely solely on their own study of the Bible. It was a time of building up and then sending them back with new zeal."

Andrzej wrote, "We would like to try to organize a small conference on Mission values, based on *Living Hope Ministries* values. We will do some research in this area and, of course, we are willing to be involved in Balkans Conference with Polish attendance. With blessings, Andrzej."

So, who knows where this will lead us? The idea of the people of these great nations coming together under one banner, that of Jesus Christ, sounds wonderful. With God in charge, the sky is the limit!

In some ways Romania is a lot like Uganda. Plenty of stray dogs wandering around, people taking care of their animals by the roadside and the roads lined with huge hoardings with brightly coloured advertisements. In 2002, my son Philip came with me to Transylvania where we even caught sight of the odd unfettered bull wandering around!

Romania has a population of some 24 million people. We started our conference in Jibou. During the journey we enjoyed going through this large country of startling beauty. It is very green and full of trees, but the people live in dull and badly maintained flats. We began the meeting at 5pm and it was still going at around midnight. On Sunday, I had the privilege of marrying a couple from the church. About 100 of us gathered as the bride and groom entered the church accompanied by the music of two accordions and an oboe, and later on we were invited to the marriage feast.

The trip was a real mixture of emotions because when we returned to Cluj I was asked to preach at a funeral service. The people had flowers, benches and a PA system outside the home of the deceased, and after a scripture reading, they brought out the coffin which was uncovered. After I had preached, the coffin was covered and taken on a horse-drawn cart to the place of burial some 2km away.

It was interesting to see the enthusiasm of the different congregations as we moved around the small villages. In a place called Mirsid, the Pastor and eighteen people had ambitions to buy a house for $2,500 to use for the church. In Bulgari we found a family hosting church in their own home, and in Ciuta the villagers had already begun to build a church, sacrificially selling their livestock to raise the funds. There was still plenty to do, but we were able to contribute a small gift. We also left clothing, glasses and other useful items donated by some of the churches in England.

CHAPTER 19

Teamwork

Now that the work of *Living Hope Ministries* has changed from being a one-man entity into an organisation, it would be good to talk about team work.

In 2007 Scott Carr led a team from Life Church to Kisumu Kenya. The team consisted of John Milborrow, Alan George, Peter Coot, Clive Culshaw and Wayne Furbur. Julie Shimizu, the minister of Life Community Baptist Church Horsham, had to change her plans at the last minute and had to postpone her visit until three weeks later. Their plan was to build a playground for the Osare Orphanage. The whole team travelled to Mathare slum. Mathare means madman, as David, their talkative taxi driver was delighted to point out because he obviously thought they were all mad to want to travel there!

Mathare has a population of nearly a million people and for the most part it is a place of utter squalor, a hot and dirty shanty town. For those going there for the first time, it was an awful shock, an emotional overload. They had to walk along narrow alleyways and warrens, crossing open sewers to greet various members of the churches. One team member described it as being like Hampton Court Maze on the wrong side of hell. But even in such horrendous conditions there is still a real hunger for the word of God and a longing for the Holy Spirit.

Moving on to Kisumu, they were greeted by some of the orphans. Scott was introduced to a man called Sammy, a candidate in the forthcoming elections from the Siaya district. Sammy had taken precious time out from campaigning to come and chat with the team.

Whilst he and Sammy sipped sodas and the team relaxed, Scott talked with and prayed for Sammy. As he prayed Scott told him that as a prospective MP, if he kept to God's ideals of anti-corruption then God would eventually raise him up to high office and enable him to bring change to the nation.

Amazingly, Scott discovered that several years back when he'd first visited Siaya, God brought the then Siayan MP to one of the pastors' meetings. Scott was speaking about how God feels about corruption in the church and in the nation. Scott had felt God prompting him to pray over the man, and that God was going to raise this politician up.

Over the years, this kind of ripple effect has become a hallmark of *Living Hope Ministries*, and for those who say that God is dead and that Christianity has no real effect on modern life… I would say, see for yourself!

James and Rose in Kisumu

The team went to the Osare Orphanage Home in Bandani (just outside Kisumu town centre) and during their stay, they made amazing progress on the project of building an adventure playground for the children. They overcame many setbacks and challenges - not least the 34°C heat (at least two members of the team suffered from heatstroke), and all of them went down with stomach problems at some point. However it was the joy and hope of the 250 children that kept them focused on the job in hand. Once on site, the team worked alongside some of the older orphans who worked hard at the digging and concreting.

Scott preached in the new Bible College building, which was only recently completed. It would have been a wonderful asset, but the leader had been a tad over ambitious. The plan had been to build a single storey building but the builders carried on and began a second floor. Unfortunately, they ran out of money and so the roof of the single storey was the floor of the yet to be built second floor. As a result, that 'roof' was open to the elements and the whole structure was in danger of serious deterioration.

We eventually decided to take a more active role in this project, so we set out some clear principles. A very generous donation alongside some locally raised funds, meant that the building could be properly completed including the roof! We have provided materials for a library and Resource Centre, which will be geared towards serious self-learning. Local people have been given the responsibility for the care of the resources provided and we have promised to provide regular teaching in seminars.

However, back in 2007, those problems had not yet come to light. A generator lit the whole hall and powered the PA and the side rooms were spacious enough to allow those pastors that travelled considerable distance to be there for the week and be able to sleep safely on site. Each day Scott had around fifty pastors and members to teach. I remember him telling me that more than ever before, there was a wonderful sense of being in the right place, at the right time and doing the right thing.

The playground was finished and for the team to see the faces of all those children and the adults as they watched from the sidelines, was something money can't buy. They had already had a lovely party day the previous Sunday, a day of feasting, celebration, photo calls and games. Now they dedicated and prayed for the new area and commissioned the Masai warriors, who acted as security for the orphanage, to take special charge of it.

The generosity of the teams is amazing. They emptied out suitcases of anything that they could possibly leave behind. Mamma Rose (Rose Kasozi) was given everything from bars of soap to First Aid kits, from t-shirts to walking boots to share among those in need. They all knew that smallest gesture would make a big impact in the lives of those in the family at Bandani. James Osare testified that no matter how many children came, the food never ran out, and now they can get fresh vegetables, fruit and even meat.

Before their flight back to Nairobi, the team spent the day just with James and Rose, and took them to the best eating place by the lake, treated them to a first class meal.

More than eighty orphans are sponsored by Life church and most of them are doing really well in school. Projects like this go a long way to convince former street children, who have already been rejected and cursed by many, that in Bandani there is a God who loves them and who welcomes them into His family.

The same year, in September, David Weaver went back out to Africa, this time to Nairobi. We planned a daytime flight so that he would get a night's sleep before commencing ministry. This was his first time in Kenya and he would be visiting Pastor John at Dandora and Pastor David at Kawangare.

As you travel from the beautiful centre of town with its gardens and lake, and the many high-rise offices along with the parliament building and Kenyatta`s mausoleum, you soon become very much aware of the rapid change in surroundings. Just a short distance away from the centre, the housing becomes drab and run-down. The streets are dirty and choked by unbelievable numbers of buses and minibuses all trying to get ahead of each other to pick the passengers up first. It's chaotic. Approaching the slum areas, first your eyes and then particularly your nose are assaulted by an incredible smell which can only be called a stink.

As soon as you think this is as bad as it gets, you turn another corner and you're suddenly faced with a rubbish tip. David had been told about all of this of course, but when he actually saw people dredging in that mass of rubbish, he was shocked.

"What were they looking for?" he asked. "Is it food? Or may be something to sell or just something that may make life just a little more bearable?"

The answer to all of those questions is, "Yes."

When he was able, David took pictures through the open window of the car but sometimes the window had to be closed because of the risk of personal injury or of the camera being snatched.

When he wrote his report back home, David said he thought Pastor John's church in Dandora was beautiful. Of course, he wasn't talking of the building, which is only a crude timber and corrugated iron structure, he was talking about the people. They don't have much of what this world offers, but they are beautiful people. For years David had sat in the pew of his local church, wishing that he could do something significant for God. He had never been an idle Christian, but he had always longed to have the chance to share the Word of God and to be of use to those in need. An ordinary man, not wealthy by any means, but David wanted to give to the Church. He had raised the funds to go out to Africa himself and his friends had contributed towards a money gift which he had for the people.

Living Hope Ministries ran a seminar on the Saturday where David spoke to a good number of pastors. Sunday morning he ministered to a congregation of at least a hundred and had the joy of seeing a number of those make a commitment to God.

The Pastors themselves live with their wives in very humble homes. It may only be two small rooms which house a family with up to six children and finding the rent to pay for this accommodation is a challenge in itself. We in the West are relatively rich in Christian heritage and in financial terms and the Lord calls us to feed the Body.

After an uneventful but expensive trip to Arusha in Tanzania, David met Pastor Nelson, the organiser of the conference, with his committee in the evening. Already it felt like the meeting of old friends, totally unlike the first visit. This time David felt a greater warmth as they greeted each other and David told me he began to wonder if his perceptions on his first visit in 2006 when he was challenged quite forcefully as to his motives for being there, were largely coloured by his own feelings of insecurity.

By 2009, a team from Elim Church Worthing, went to Rwanda for the fifth time. Bishop Augustine Gakwaya welcomed Bernard Lord, Jenny Quaife and Jim McCue and as on previous visits, they stayed at the Havugimana Israel conference centre and guest house, part of the headquarters of the African Evangelical Enterprise (AEE). This is an African organisation based in Kigali that is dedicated to spreading the Gospel throughout Africa and it serves as a stopping off /meeting point for all sorts of Christian organisations and churches as well as Christian mission workers from all over the world.

Over the five year period that the *Living Hope Ministries* team had been visiting Rwanda, they noticed the change in the local conditions and the infrastructure within Kigali. Tarmac roads were continuing to be extended away from the commercial and government heart of Kigali and out into the suburbs. The road system has changed from churned-up, crater-strewn 'battle field' conditions to western standard roads. There has been land clearance on a massive scale and slum areas have continued to be cleared. Bernard told me that for the first time, they saw what must have been over a hundred people reworking the land in an areas where just two years previously there had been congested, slum condition homes. The district roads range from being extremely poor, to sometimes dangerous (by western standards) but still the driving standards have to be seen to be believed. However, the general road worthiness of vehicles, now that there is a form of MOT in operation, has however greatly improved. I recall Bernard telling me that on his first visit to Rwanda in 2005, he was collected from Kigali airport by a pastor whose vehicle had no dashboard, no handbrake, no windscreen, and holes in the floor so big he could see the road passing beneath his feet!

On their first evening in Kigali the members of the team were welcomed into the home of their host, Bishop Augustine Gakwaya. It is a humble dwelling for a man with such great responsibilities and influence in the church. Built on a slope, from his home you can see Kigali airport in the distance. In between, are the homes of the people he serves in the area. After so many years of coming to Rwanda, the teams from *Living Hope Ministries* not only enjoy seeing familiar faces but they are welcomed by people who now treat them as true friends.

As in previous years the team began by visiting the Kisozi Genocide Memorial site in Kigali. It holds the remains of 250,000 people and plays a major part in explaining the events that led up to the genocide that took place throughout Rwanda in 1994. This and other sites that they visited, such as the Ntarama Memorial site, are open to every Rwandan, including school children, as well as foreign visitors. The Rwandan people are determined that the mistakes of the past will not be forgotten and to that end, they have an active policy of education for everyone. These sites are a shocking indictment of what men and women are capable of doing to each other because of envy, prejudice and hatred, but it's not only in Africa that these things happen. There are rooms within the memorial site dedicated to the victims of the Holocaust, the ethnic cleansing in Bosnia and other places where genocide has taken place.

It is a measure of the ever-growing influence of the Christian faith and the Christian message supported by the government, that people are now able to live together as Rwandans and refer to one another as Rwandan, and not as once was the norm, remaining separate as Hutu or Tutsi.

Although in some parts of the world Christianity gets a bad press, the churches in Rwanda are working together, preaching forgiveness and love and serving the people in many positive ways. This is arguably the most important means by which Rwanda has managed to overcome its hundred days of genocide in which an estimated one million Tutsi and moderate Hutu people were killed, a shocking statistic which was approximately 10,000 murders a day.

The programme of church visits for the team was a very busy one. At certain times they were entertained by church choirs. These are truly magnificent, and with their lovely harmonies, they rival choirs anywhere in the world. Having said that, the combination of singing, rhythmic clapping and stamping of the people in ordinary church services as they praised God, was at times dramatic, beautiful and very moving especially considering the fact that most of the churches are very poor.

For the third successive year the team was invited to be on local Christian radio. Quite exciting to know that Bernard's message could be heard by over two million listeners tuned in to the radio.

The team met with the widows and others that they had been able to help over the previous five years. Quite a few have now benefited from the Widows' Revolving Fund that they set up in 2005. One young man was also given the sum of £50 provided by the team to start a very modest barbershop in a poor district of Kigali. When they visited him they were very pleased to see that his business was progressing so well that he was able to send support to his family back in his own village.

These schemes are not funded by *Living Hope Ministries*, but I am more than happy for those who have a burden for the people to help in whatever way they can. I have to be very careful not to get sidetracked by a cause no matter how worthwhile or worthy it may seem. God called me to preach the word and to get teaching and teaching aids, particularly Bibles, into the hands of impoverished Pastors and Leaders. The wonderful thing is, God has supplied for their physical needs as well. It doesn't have to be either or. God has made sure it's both. Different people have different callings.

Once again the team renewed their links with the local orphanage and Annoncieta, the housemother. On this occasion they were able to help financially with the running costs by providing money for food.

Sometimes people take on a special need. For instance, Terry Griffiths supports a young family on a monthly basis. The husband, Innocent Nizeyimana, was heavily into witchcraft and its practices and consequently became infected with HIV. It was through accepting Christ as his Saviour and turning his life around that he started to put his faith into action. As in previous visits to Africa, the team saw first-hand people who had been saved from the very real destructive power of witchcraft.

The whole ECF team, which includes a small dedicated fund-raising committee at home, has managed, through various events, to raise money for the purchase of land for the church in Kigali, for the purpose of growing pineapples. In 2009, they tasted their first pineapple from the pineapple field and although the church has had to employ a 'learning by doing' approach, they were able to discuss with the Church leader the next step in the development of the field.

The most recent and ambitious project that the ECF team has successfully completed has been the purchase of a minibus. This has enabled the church to ferry its older people to and from church as well as being put to use during the week in the local community which brings in funds for the church.

The previous year the team had been given a donation of £120 so that they could put on a party for the children in the orphanage. There was also a donation for the purchase of Bibles. On their latest trip, they were again given another donation of £100 for the purchase of Bibles and they bought fifteen Bibles in the Kinyarwanda language in Rwanda rather than shipping them from the UK. By doing that, the Christian bookshop in Kigali gets some much needed business.

The projects for this small church seem to get bigger. The team has agreed to raise the sum of £10-£18,000 so that a Bible school can be built. It is hoped that the students will eventually go back into the provinces and the local communities. To that end, in 2009 they decided to take a step of faith and open a charity shop in Worthing. Faith Through Action has become well established and the profits are ploughed into projects like this.

As their 2009 visit came to a close, the team was invited by one of the church elders to his home for a meal. There they met an old man, the father of our host. The old man could not speak English but kept staring at the team members as everybody talked and had their meal. Later on he asked his son how he had managed to get white people to come to his home and to eat with the family and to get on with one another so well! The old man praised God for what he had seen, because in his day, no white person would do such a thing.

I remember once asking David Weaver, "Who got the most blessing?"

"It has to be me," he said.

We are all united in Christ and where God is, there is blessing. Isn't that what it's all about?

The team keeps growing: the administrative team to keep us well organised and prepared on a practical level, the teaching team built around Chris Lane, the pastors from churches and myself. The Africa team, The Europe team built around Andrzej and Zeljko, The prayer team, Praise God for the many who regularly pray and lift up to the Lord the ministry of Living Hope and the growing number of churches showing real interest in the ministry. Everyone is vital; all are appreciated but more are needed.

CHAPTER 20

Moving On

———————

To sum up the last fifteen years would be quite difficult. Those years have been peppered with opportunities to serve the Lord in so many places. I've been able to share the gospel and it's been amazing to see people coming to Christ in so many nations. I have been protected in difficult situations and from dangers and illness. I have stories of fantastic healings, and stories about people whose lives have been transformed by hearing the word of God. As I've attempted to share some of these things, I've realised that it's impossible to include everything. I've had to leave out so much. I wish I could have told you about everyone, but perhaps I can include them in another book because the story of *Living Hope Ministries* hasn't ended yet. God is still using us, and more and more Christians are coming alongside us to help.

So many have contributed to *Living Hope Ministries* behind the scenes. I am so grateful for all of them. They have sacrificed in terms of time, money and prayer. Doris Russell who died at the age of 102 in 2009, was a massively supportive lady. She came out to the meetings in Croydon until she was 98, and she was still going to Hangleton when she was 101.

Doris' dearest friend Nora Holdstock now in her nineties herself, and living in Koinonia the same Christian care home where Doris lived, is still supportive and a great prayer warrior. I am sure people like that have a surprise in store when they go to be with the Lord. Unsung heroes on earth, they must be the toast of heaven.

People talk about great men of God but I prefer to talk about the great God of men. In 1994 God was pouring out his blessings and spiritually speaking, I fell into a rapidly flowing river. This whole adventure hasn't been about me. It was only the current that carried me along. I give Him all the glory and the honour.

Family Celebration

My family, as you will already have seen from previous pages have been the most amazingly supportive people. Elaine and each of my sons have given of themselves to serve *Living Hope Ministries* in whatever way they can and now my two daughters-in-law have followed. My mother and my brother and the wider members of the family… they are just as great.

Matt, our third son, is a sensitive man with a lot of enthusiasm. He may find it challenging to be a Christian in this modern world but he works hard at his job in the plumbing department of a hardware store and loves the Lord. So often, Matt will pray with me. In fact, when I ring from whichever country I happen to be in, Matt will always offer to pray with me over the phone and he's always sending me text messages which are full of support.

I went to Korea when Jon was very young and Elaine told me that one day he picked up the telephone in the bedroom and said, "Daddy, I haven't seen you for thousands and thousands of years."

When I came home, I used to meet him from school and we used to go to a photographic shop together to collect the photographs I had taken on the trips. Jon always wanted a picture of where I slept. I had spent upwards of £1,000, been to some fantastic sounding places in exotic sounding countries but all he wanted to see was a crumpled pillow and some sheets! He is now as keen as mustard to come on mission with me and after his first trip to Africa, his life was transformed. Sometimes, if I pop my head around his bedroom door, he's there reading his Bible.

Jon came with me to Nigeria in 2009. He was in his element teaching in the school and the Sunday School where he taught the children The Lord's Prayer. They all enjoyed many happy hours singing songs and listening to Jon telling them stories.

When Phil was quite young, he stepped out in front of a car, which threw him in the air and he landed on the bonnet. We thanked God that he wasn't badly hurt or even killed. A conscientious man, Phil has Elaine's temperament. When he came with me on trips, he handled difficulties and problems in exactly the same way as she would.

My oldest son, Paul, supports me in other ways. I just have to give him a call and he willingly runs around London sorting out the visas I need, and Julia, my other daughter-in-law, married to Phil, does all the Sunday school notes which we put onto the website. Steve mentioned elsewhere, is so encouraging in prayer and support.

We not only have teams going out to various parts of the globe but we also have friends of *Living Hope Ministries* in diverse places. For instance, Dave and Claire Richards have agreed to co-ordinate our new found links in New Zealand and will seek to establish other links as God leads. They attend a lively church in Tawa. Dave and Claire are good friends and have worked with us over the years in other settings. Now in New Zealand, they write, "We have had some good feedback from Johnsonville. One lady has rung me up and wants to meet for coffee to discuss *Living Hope Ministries*. We will look into having a prayer meeting at the beginning of the month to pray for *Living Hope Ministries* and will be gradually following up interested contacts. Our Corps officers Dave and Judith have asked us at some stage to write an article for the church magazine about our responsibilities with *Living Hope Ministries*. At one of the meetings we arranged for Richard, there was a prophecy about God opening the door to Ecuador, South America." 2011, by the grace of God we will see that visit. It is amazing how God keeps opening the doors to serve Him."

We are amazed that even after all these years, people we have known as friends still rally round the banner of *Living Hope Ministries*. People from our Norfolk days, West Hoathly days, to Brighton days, Grace Church days and now in Lancing have really supported us. Although I have an itinerate ministry, I don't always talk about *Living Hope Ministries*. I am primarily a preacher of the Word. I make a clear distinction between the two. If I am asked to speak on *Living Hope Ministries* then I do. Of course, if I am asked I have a ready answer. Even now, many people think *Living Hope Ministries* is an organisation I work for and I take some pleasure in their lack of understanding. It tells me that I have not pushed myself to the fore.

I have had introductions to other churches through conversations with pastors in the field. I was the first white man to preach in Pastor Owolabi's church in London. They have taken a real interest in the work in India and are very supportive to the ministry.

My early visits were fraught with the problems of making telephone contact with Elaine back home. Landlines were often unreliable and in some places you were supposed to pay a bribe to secure one. The advent of the mobile phone in Africa brought about massive change. The ability to contact someone even in the poorest of areas was a remarkable step forward. For the first time I was able to stand outside a mud hut, which was to be my home for the night, and listen to Elaine's prayers and encouragement.

Texting or sending an sms is an acquired skill, but I am now able to be in touch with friends all over the world.

A close call to a tragedy was to inspire a ministry which still seems a little bizarre. It happened when terrorists planted a bomb in a package near Glasgow airport. The device had been set up so that a call to a mobile phone hidden within the package, would trigger the bomb to explode. Praise the Lord the device failed but I began to think of ways in which we should use the mobile phone for good.

Thus it was that I began speaking to places far and wide using the mobile phone. I rang from my garage in Lancing, England, which had been converted into an office. When my friends answered their phones, they would switch on the speaker button and amplify my voice for the people attending the meeting. The person receiving the message would, if necessary, interpret what I was saying and it became like a live radio programme. Using this tool, *Living Hope Ministries* has addressed many conferences in far flung places. When a meeting is arranged it's not just to hear me but there is worship, testimony and other speakers. I am a part of the programme not the sum total of it but it also means that when I am needed in another place, or if a conference has been left in charge of a friend of the ministry, I can still be involved from home.

We have used the mobile phone during crusades in Sierra Leone for a few years now and the numbers attending those meetings have been in the thousands. Reports of conversions and healings are regular and eye-witnesses testify to the grace of God. Every Saturday, we teach in a Bible school and in conferences in Ethiopia by this method. I regularly receive reports and pictures of what's been happening. Praise the Lord! We are able to get good mobile phone rates which means calls are very reasonably priced. Certainly a lot cheaper than the airfare!

When we minister, we must minister by faith not by sight. By God's grace words of knowledge and insight come as one preaches and God always honours His word. It's great to be able to support others and to enhance their ministries in this way.

We have a gift day once a year and people are very generous.

In 2002 Tim Clarke from Lancing Tabernacle offered to set up the Website for *Living Hope Ministries*. This has been a great blessing and benefit. Gradually, countries connected with *Living Hope Ministries* have made it a lot more meaningful by their contributions. For example Pastor Toni Mrvic from Slovenia has taken the time to write a whole page about his own church, its history, its hopes and requests for prayer. We are always looking for new ways in which we can serve the church and as mentioned we now have a children's Bible Study which has been created by our daughter-in-law, Julia Brunton.

Tim's work kept him very busy so now Paul Bettelley maintains the website in his spare time. We have had more than 51,000 hits. It is regularly updated and you can hear a radio broadcast, see the *Living Hope Ministries* diary, and scroll down to read up-to-date information about the country you're interested in.

I love it when people who long to serve the Lord take opportunities like this. Paul is so excited when he sees the fruit of his efforts.

One way traffic is never satisfying.

In 2009 I celebrated my 60th birthday and to my great surprise, people gathered from all over the country for a party. I had a vague idea something was going on but the number of folks in that room took my breath away. Some were relatives, my mother, my younger brother Michael, and my children, but the guest list included aunts, cousins and other family members and close friends. There were people I'd worked with at school when I first became a teacher, people from my days with Terry Virgo, some members of the Board of Trustees, people who had been on missions with me, or without me, my home church pastor, the list was endless. I have been truly blessed because each one knew my position and what I stood for. Even if they didn't all share the same denomination, there is something about *Living Hope Ministries* which has caught their imagination over the years. I am immensely grateful to them and most of all I am eternally grateful to God for what He has done. You may remember the incident in West Africa which began this story.

We had been summoned to appear before the police to answer questions about our motives as we drove along the streets taking photographs. One in snapshot particular was causing concern. My son Jonni had leaned out of the car window and taken a picture of what we later discovered was a government building.

At nine o'clock sharp, we arrived at the police station and were interviewed. We tried to make it plain that we had no intention of harming the people of their nation. On the contrary, we told them, we loved the people and through the churches, we were trying to help those on the fringes of society. At one point two of our interrogators looked at each other and said, "What are we doing?"

I thought it was over but once again, we were taken to a room to wait. The Pastor was taken back into detention.

After a while, a very senior church minister, a personal friend of our host, turned up. He had been summoned to speak for us, which he did. In fact, he seemed convinced that someone was making mischief.

Eventually someone with more rank appeared with an apology and we were finally allowed to go. When we got the camera back, they had deleted a number of other pictures.

We had prayed, putting the whole situation into God's hands and once again, He had not let us down. We are often impatient, wanting things sorted and sorted right now. God has his timing and we have to trust Him.

To Him be all glory and honour! Thank you, Jesus.

CHAPTER 21

The Most Important Choice of your Life

When I became a Christian at the age of thirteen, from that moment on, I had a burden to lead others to Christ. There was a crusade in the Baptist Church in Fakenham just after I got saved and I trained to be a counsellor. The material they used was from a Billy Graham course. I was a bit young to be released as a counsellor but they gave me the training and subsequently, when I was fourteen, I had the privilege of leading a young man to Christ at a Bible camp. I was so excited. It was an amazing experience.

So how do we lead someone to Christ?

The first thing is that the person should know that they are a sinner and that they need God's forgiveness.

Romans 3 v. 23 *For all have sinned and fall short of the glory of God…*

This is everybody's predicament and there are no excuses. Every single one of us has fallen short of God's perfect standard.

The second thing to be aware of is that when we sin, there is a consequence.

Romans 6 v. 23 *For the wages of sin is death…*

We understand from Hebrews 9v 27 *Man is destined to die once, and after that to face judgment.*

Sin separates us from God. As a result, we do not have a sense of destiny, no confidence regarding what will happen when we die and often no peace and purpose in our lives. Unless that penalty can be removed, it means that we will not only be separate from God now, but forever separated in a place the Bible calls hell. What is hell? It is being in the darkness, unaware of anybody else, totally isolated and desperate for some sense of love and help. But sadly, help is not coming. This is an eternal state.

It is important to know that hell was not made for man; it was made for the devil. Satan is very keen to have as many as possible in hell with him which is why he constantly entices us to be disobedient to God.

It is important to understand that although we cannot save ourselves or earn forgiveness, or even make any improvement in our condition, the Grace of God has been at work.

Ephesians 2 v. 8, 9 *For it is by grace you have been saved, through faith-and this not from yourselves, it is the gift of God- not by works, so that no one can boast.*

When God in His mercy, grace and love saw our awful predicament, our fatal disease, He was willing to do something to rescue us from sin and its consequences. We will not understand salvation or forgiveness until we have come to the end of ourselves completely and recognise that we cannot do anything to get ourselves right with God.

God has come Himself, in the person of Christ, to deal with our sin.

Romans 5 v. 8 *But God demonstrates his own love for us in this: While we were still sinners, Christ died for us.*

John 3 v. 16 *For God so loved the world (put your name there) that he gave his one and only Son, that whoever believes in him shall not perish but have eternal life.*

1 Peter 2 v. 24 *He himself bore our sins in his body on the tree, so that we might die to sins and live for righteousness...*

Christ has died for us and once we put our confidence in that, then God can forgive us. Christ has answered any accusation the devil may make with regard to our sin. In the death of Christ, there is cleansing and forgiveness for all that we've done. We can have a clean start, a fresh new life.

It is good to acknowledge we're sinners and that Christ died for us because we couldn't save ourselves but there is a further step. We must receive Christ. We must consciously invite Him to come into our lives.

John 1 v. 12 *Yet to all who received him, to those who believed in his name, he gave the right to become children of God.*

Romans 19 v. 9 *That if you confess with your mouth, "Jesus is Lord," and believe in your heart that God raised him from the dead, you will be saved.*

When we accept Him and invite Him into our lives, God makes us brand new people inside.

Having received Christ, the Word of God (The Bible) tells us that it's important to be baptised. This is not just a ritual but a powerful demonstration that you've turned your back on the old, that you've truly repented for your sins, and you want to live a new life. It's a wonderful way to demonstrate that your old life has now gone and your new life is with Christ.

Baptism speaks of the death and resurrection of Christ. As we go under the water, we are identifying with Christ, saying, 'He died for me.' As we are lifted out of the water, we are identifying with Christ in His resurrection.

It is also important that as we surrender our lives to Christ, we are filled with the Holy Spirit. The early Christians understood that Jesus died for them and that He'd risen from the dead. They knew that He ascended into heaven to pray for them and that He sent the Holy Spirit to give them power. We too can ask the Holy Spirit to fill us.

Acts 1v 8 *But you will receive power when the Holy Spirit comes on you; and you will be my witnesses in Jerusalem, and in all Judea and Samaria, and to the ends of the earth.*

We can receive the self-same Holy Spirit that they received and this will enable us to be witnesses for Christ. We can boldly proclaim who He is. Receiving the Holy Spirit also opens the door to spiritual gifts which help us to play our part in the body of Christ (fellow believers in Christ) and to build them up.

A simple prayer which has been for many the opening of a door to let Jesus come in, goes like this:

Lord Jesus,
I realise that I am a sinner. I realise that if this situation continues,
I'll be eternally separate from you. I'm asking you to forgive me
because sin has messed up my life and I want to be a new person.
I also ask your forgiveness because I want to go to heaven and not to
hell. I know I deserve hell. I couldn't argue with you if that's where
I ended up, but you have died for me so that I can go to heaven.
So Lord Jesus, I turn my back on sin. I don't want to live life without
you any more. I want you to come into my life and to take charge.
I promise that from this day I want to live under your Lordship.
I want to live to please you. Thank you, Jesus,
Amen.

If you have prayed that prayer, do get in touch with us and tell us. We'd like to send you some literature to help you.

Rev. Richard Brunton
Living Hope Ministries
www.living-hope.org.uk
email : lhm@living-hope.org.uk

CHAPTER 22

The Final Word
from Bishop Stephen Kiguru

L*iving Hope* began in Kenya Africa and has now spread to Europe, Asia, New Zealand and South America, all by God's grace. However let the final word go to my good friend Bishop Stephen Kiguru from Kenya . As early visits were on my own, I began to stay at his home. What a privilege! I remember prayers at breakfast where thanking God for keeping us safe through the night took on a new reality. It was not

Bishop Stephen Kiguru

taken for granted to see the next day at all but a genuine appreciation that life is in his hands. I am always touched by prayers at the meal table which always include those who have nothing. I have learned so much from this godly couple. Stephen's counsel and wisdom have been a great source of strength. Stephen has had great responsibility in Kenya once being the overseer of a movement covering 2000 churches over the whole of Kenya. He has pioneered many projects bringing a level of integrity and accountability which has made some enemies but has abundantly pleased our Saviour. He founded the Great Commission churches of Tanzania and plans even in retirement to serve them and LHM.

At a *Living Hope* Day in London in 2010, he sent an appreciation of the development of LHM which is very humbling but a powerful testimony of God's grace. Here is a summary of the key points.

Christianity in Africa has a history of about 200 years when England sent its young men and women, energetic, well- educated and professionally trained, who sailed through the vast waters of the Atlantic and Indian oceans carrying Christ to the then Dark continent. *Missionaries preached and taught the Word of God. Africans were converted and trained to reach further areas. This went on despite the dryness of the sermons, until the wake of the Pentecostal movement, which brought unexpected heavy revival in the same churches, causing confusion and disrupting their orders of service through the outpouring of the Holy Spirit evidenced by the speaking in tongues, prophecies and other miracles.*

This act of the Holy Spirit resulted in excommunications from the churches which paved the way for the birth of the Pentecostal churches. The fire burned far and wide.

Between the mid 60's and 80's, these churches had grown numerously and geographically but lacked sound teachings in the Word of God. The result was shallow pastors who could hardly ground their members. In a Christian leadership magazine, someone wrote, 'African Christianity is 100 miles long, but only 1inch deep.'

Being unaware of what was happening many preachers sprang up with distorted messages about salvation, the Holy Spirit, speaking in tongues, prophecies and miracles.

These heretic preachers were born from major crusades organized by both local and international evangelists, but were not spiritually matured, and left on their own like orphans, who spiritually fed on any doctrine - a little here, a little there, whether right or wrong. They imitated the evangelist who preached to them - in style of preaching, style of dressing, the way he held his Bible and his English accent.

Through such behaviours the Church of Christ has been embarrassed and ridiculed, creating doubts on whether the evangelicals/Pentecostals have run short of the truth of the Word of God. Many pastors/preachers were hanging onto imaginary and commercial sermons that scare, manipulate and exploit their congregations in terms of giving.

Many churches are full on Sundays with good choirs, much praising and worshipping and jubilations, but feeding on sermons full of heresies.

Rev. Brunton first stepped on African soil in 1994. He began by attending conferences followed by preaching in churches. He received invitations to speak in churches in the slums of Nairobi and pastors were attracted by his teachings. After travelling to different parts of Kenya, he settled down, holding pastors' conferences on his own, having been welcomed in a full gospel church where he brought together Pastors from the slums of Nairobi and some from Western Kenya. As the membership grew rapidly, he divided the conferences into several other areas of Nairobi; Kisumu, Mombasa and Arusha in Tanzania. To date the African ministry covers Kenya, Tanzania, Uganda, Rwanda, Malawi, Sudan, Congo DRC, Nigeria, Sierra Leone and of late Burundi.

While many western preachers coming to Africa invite pastors to big hotels for meals and other things, Rev. Brunton has persistently maintained his vision and focus to the less privileged pastors in the neglected slums of the above named countries. To the best of my knowledge the pastors can fit into the following categories:

* neglected by seniors for economical reasons
* spiritually illegitimate,
* spiritual orphans,
* runaway/estranged because of harsh working conditions or for personal interests, but coming to their senses eventually. However they lack the courage to rejoin their former churches or ministries.

My understanding and experience tell me that God has given Richard favours by touching men and women, old and young from England, to join him in his mission trips. The number of these volunteers has been growing from time to time. We in Africa, thank God for these different teams. They have blessed us in many ways. The volunteers/mission teams have accomplished much including the following:

- Bible exposition - this has given much light and good ground to many pastors who have no good study bibles
- Leadership - introducing pastors to sound church governance, church management and administration, finance management, economic empowerment, stewardship etc. - Trips to new and remote areas offering pastoral services as well as encouraging pastors.
- Humanitarian services have also been assisted and Bibles in English, Swahili and French have been distributed to many pastors in the above countries.

As we introduce LHM in new areas of East and Central Africa, we are emphatic on the six (6) pillars that the ministry is built upon:

1. Prayer
2. Word of God
3. Fellowship
4. Unity
5. Reconciliation
6. Proclamation

Having been one of the spenders of the ministry's money, I know huge sums are spent every year. However the labours are not in vain. In East and Central Africa alone, over 1000 church leaders are reached every year. Sudan and Burundi are our new establishments and these leaders represent an average of 50, 000 Christians.

For prayer purposes, it is important to note that the above countries are among the poorest in Africa, where the average income per person per day is 0.75 dollars.

Living Hope Ministries is an apostolic ministry and is in Africa "on time". Having seen what God has done through this ministry, we have no doubt about the clarity of the vision and Rev. Richard Brunton's focus on greater heights and achievements. Many foreign ministers coming to Africa have broken up relationships both with their recipients/hosts as well as fellow ministers. Competitions have been experienced with missionaries who finally segregate poor African pastors who innocently join a chorus without detecting the consequences. Thank God for the existing program of prayers on the first Friday of every month. The results are evident. However, for further propagation and sustainability of the ministry, churches and concerned individuals must fervently pray without ceasing. Holding high the hands of Richard and Elaine, just as Aaron and Hur did when Moses and Joshua won the battle.

In conclusion, may I summarise my remarks in a few words:

- God is visiting Africa again through LHM after the break with CMS.
- God is raising churches in England (not denominations) to finish the task in Africa.
- God has raised LHM as an apostolic ministry to restore the fading glory in the African churches".

Bishop Stephen Kiguru

Prologue

God so loved the world that he gave Jesus. The sacrifice of Jesus dying on the cross for us is the greatest act of love that God could reveal. It is the prime motivation for my ministry that Christ loved me and gave Himself for me. The nations are very much on God's heart and now by His wonderful grace, the nations are on my heart too. Let us reach out with the gospel of Jesus to all the world and see churches planted and led by godly leaders that point people to Jesus our only Living Hope.

By God's grace Bishop Stephen and other African team members plan a special service to recognise the ministry in January 2012. Several nations will be represented. It is very humbling and kind but the greatest thing of all is to hear, one day, my Lord Jesus say

"Well done good and faithful servant!".

To God be the glory great things He has done!

APPENDIX

Travel Tips

The purpose of this book has been to share the wonderful things God has done through Living Hope Ministries. Along the way we have picked up a great many useful tips and handy hints to help the traveller. What follows is not a comprehensive list of dos and donts but it may help to clarify any leanings toward third world travel with a view to mission. Other groups will have their particular advice but I hope this may be of use:

- Check with the website of the country of your destination to find out what medication is needed. Some drugs are available on the National Health but you will have to pay for others. You will not be allowed in some countries if you have not had the appropriate injections.

When packing your hand luggage for the plane, be sure to include:
- On long haul flights wear travel socks or stockings.
- A spare set of underwear.
- A book or some other reading material.
- Something warm, a cardigan or jumper (especially if on a night flight).
- A small bag of toiletries but remember, no liquids over 100ml.
- Keep all valuables, your camera, mobile, money, jewellery, passport and travel documents with you.
- Keep a photocopy of your passport separately in case you accidentally lose it.

- If you are likely to use your mobile phone while abroad, consider buying a local SIM card.

- Take a small first aid kit which includes antiseptic cream, over the counter painkillers, plasters, and mosquito spray containing Deet. Check the advice given with regard to other pills, on the website of the country of your destination. For example, some countries ban the use of birth control pills.
- Take some dehydration sachets. If you do become overheated, you can very quickly lose body salts. Drinking plenty may not be enough. A dehydration sachet will soon restore the chemical balance of your body.
- A small travel sewing kit is always handy.
- A torch with new batteries.
- Toiletries.
- Bath towel. You can buy a travel towel which will pack up very small but it is actually quite large.
- When choosing your clothing, if you are going to a hot country, cotton is best. Take some tops with long sleeves which are handy in the evenings when the mosquitoes are about.
- If on a Christian mission, remember to take some suitable clothing for church.
- Men may need a tie and women should dress conservatively. In the more rural areas, African women tend not to wear trousers, especially not in church but for western visitors it is generally not seen as a problem. Trousers will protect your legs from mosquito bites.
- Sandals/shoes suitable for walking.
- When staying in a hotel/guest house mosquito nets should be provided, but when staying with people in their own homes, take your own net. It is better not to take a chance.
- Consider taking gifts for your host and family. Look at your planned itinerary or visits and take gifts as appropriate. In most third world countries, a little money goes a long way.
- Take sufficient money to cover your accommodation, food, travel and gifts. Use a money belt worn next to the skin.

- Take some teaching aids, your notes if appropriate, a Bible, writing material.
- Have a bag or wallet for daily use. Do not go around with valuables in a backpack unless the zips and fastenings are next to your back. An over the shoulder bag is better.

Each country has its own requirements when it comes to vaccinations. It is advisable to see your doctor at least six weeks before you plan to go on your short term mission. Sometimes you must have a period of time between injections in order for them to take effect.

For instance, when travelling to East Africa you will need:

- *Yellow Fever:* Once you have had this vaccination, you will be issued with a certificate which you should carry at all times with your passport. It is valid for ten years.
- *Typhoid:* The typhoid vaccine is given in two doses with four to six weeks in between. It gives you immunity for up to three years.
- *Tetanus:* The Department of Health recommends having a booster dose to this disease at ten year intervals.
- *Hepatitis A:* Hepatitis A is associated with poor hygiene and sanitation. A single dose of the vaccine will give you immunity for up to one year. If you are likely to be travelling more than once, you can get immunity from Hepatitis A for up to ten years with a booster dose given between six and twelve months of the original dose.

- Malaria is transferred to humans from the bite of a mosquito infected with the parasite. There is a high risk in East Africa. All travellers should take one of the following drugs: malarone, atovaquone/proguanil, doxycycline, mefloquine, or primaquine (in special circumstances). Seek the advice of your GP. Continue to take your antimalarial drug for four weeks (mefloquine or doxycycline) or seven days (atovaquone/proguanil) after your return to the UK.

- Travellers' diarrhoea is caused by viruses, bacteria, or parasites. Avoid buying food or drink from street vendors and always drink bottled water from a reputable source.
- It is advisable not to swim in fresh water, except in well-chlorinated swimming pools.
- An oral vaccine is available in the UK for travellers to endemic or epidemic areas, where the risk of cholera is greatest. In most cases, a cholera vaccination certificate is no longer required.
- Meningococcal meningitis is more common in some areas of Africa and Asia than in the UK. A vaccine is available to protect against some strains. Saudi Arabia requires all pilgrims during the Hajj to be vaccinated.
- If you haven't been vaccinated against TB and are staying for more than a month in Eastern Europe, Asia, Africa, Central or South America, you should consider a Bacille Calmette-Guerin (BCG) vaccination. Preferably, this should be given at least two months before departure.

- Try to avoid unpasteurised dairy products.
- Wearing long sleeves and long trousers is the best way to avoid ticks. Tuck your trousers into your socks. Stay on trails as much as possible and avoid brush. Infected ticks are found on forest fringes with adjacent grassland, forest glades, riverside meadows and marshland, forest plantations with brushwood, and shrubbery. They reside most commonly on ground level vegetation, on the underside of foliage, from where they can be brushed onto clothing or drop onto passing humans.
- A DEET-based insect repellent is a must. Look for something that says it repels ticks. It you can't find that, go for something with 20-50% DEET. Once you get over 50% DEET, you really don't gain much in effectiveness and you do increase chances for problems. You may be intolerant to

higher concentration of DEET and it may damage plastics. Inspect your clothing and body for ticks after hiking each day. If you have a travelling companion, have them check out your back or other spots you can't see.

* As soon as you arrive at your destination, make it a priority to find out how to summon help in the case of an emergency, or better still, use the Internet before you go. In the UK you dial 999 but there is no world-wide standardised emergency number. For example, in Poland you dial 997 for the police, or if calling from a mobile telephone the number is 112. The ambulance service is the familiar 999 whereas the Fire Brigade is 998. In Kenya it's 999 for all emergencies and in Bosnia 112 for all Emergencies

* You may have problems with the local electricity supply in Africa. There may be frequent power cuts and you may need to take voltage and plug adaptors.

Praying for the people

Praising people

Baptising people

APPENDIX

An Example of a Monthly Bible Study

Joshua Chapter 3: You have never been this way before

Here is an amazing chapter, where God's people cross the river Jordan and see a miracle similar to the crossing of the Red Sea. Joshua takes the lead and the priests have a key role to play. God's people then follow the example set before them. Again, the strategy and initiative come from the Lord and it requires faith and obedience to carry out His will.

You have never been this way before (v4)

So often, to move forward and see the blessings that God desires for us, will require new steps of faith. It's necessary to avoid standing still and resting on the past. The ark was a powerful symbol of God's presence. To follow the ark, was to follow the Lord. God's presence with the people was not to be taken for granted and healthy respect is called for. Today, we enjoy God's grace and promises but we too must be careful to avoid running ahead or lagging behind our Lord Jesus.

Consecrate yourselves (v5)

Joshua is confident that the Lord is about to do amazing things and so he urges the people to rededicate their lives to God. It is always good to check how much we are moving in the flesh and human reasoning, thinking of our own comforts, and how much we are fully surrendered to the Lord.

Joshua is told that the Lord will begin to exalt him (v7), to demonstrate that He is with him, as He was with Moses. How important it is, for the Lord to lift up those he chooses. If we lift ourselves up, if we strive for the attention that we think we deserve, we will fail and it will only bring misery.

Joshua tells the priests to step into the Jordan with the ark, even though it is in full flow – in fact, at flood levels! Jesus always goes before us! Whatever we face, He has faced it first. That is why He went to the cross. There is no suffering, challenge or pain that He cannot identify with. Joshua tells the people to choose one person from each tribe. Their work is described in Chapter 4, where we learn that they are each to pick up a stone from the river bed and place it later as a memorial. The priests had the role of offering sacrifices on behalf of the people. One priest went into the holiest place in the temple, to offer sacrifice and prayer, once a year. All Christian leadership must have a priestly role. We do not, in any way, want to rob people of their own walk and relationship with God – there is a priesthood of all believers. However, leaders have the privilege of seeking God on behalf of his people and we have the responsibility to take the first steps and to set an example in all things.

The water dries up (v15-17)

As soon as the priest's feet touch the water, then the water from upstream in the river Jordan dries up. The priests stand on dry ground in the middle of the river, while the people cross. This must have taken some considerable time and the priests must have been very tired. However, they did not move until the crossing was complete. Leaders especially, need to hold their ground. We do get tired and weary. The weight of leadership is heavy – but the Lord is our strength!

So, let us be courageous and realise that we are often in a place of life and ministry, where we have not been before. This is very true for ourselves in Living Hope Ministries. We must avoid complacency and recognise that, however sincere and devout our commitment to Christ might have been in the past, for each one of us the issue always has to be, "Where am I now?" – in terms of loving Christ, keeping from sin and pursuing only His will!

The nature of leadership means that we uphold and handle things, for the benefit of those we lead. It is, in fact, a privilege to 'hold the ark', while others press onward but the most important thing of all to know, is that Jesus is standing in the 'river' for us. He has taken our sin and he has died our death. Many think of the river Jordan as a picture of passing through death to new life. Jesus has conquered death and has opened up a new and living way for us!

Praise the Lord!

Rev. Richard Brunton

Living Hope Ministries exists to build the church
through teaching and informed advice, training and evangelism
within a network of churches and leaders in the
UK, Africa, Europe, Asia and other regions as called by God.

One Name One Number
The Story of *Living Hope Ministries*
Richard Brunton (with Pam Weaver)
4 Carisbrooke Close, Lancing, West Sussex BN15 0HF
email: lhm@living-hope.org.uk